BANANA

THE TRUE STORY OF HOW A **DEMEANING NICKNAME**

MAN

OPENED **AMAZING DOORS** FOR THE GOSPEL

RAY COMFORT

Bridge-Logos
Newberry, Florida 32669

Banana Man: The true story of how a demeaning nickname opened amazing doors for the gospel

Published by:
Bridge-Logos
Newberry, Florida 32669, USA
www.bridgelogos.com

Printed in the United States of America

Library of Congress Control Number: 2017931022

ISBN 978-1-61036-193-4

Unless otherwise indicated, Scripture quotations are from the New King James Version. Copyright © 1982 by Thomas Nelson, Inc. Used by permission. All rights reserved.

Scripture quotations designated KJV are from the King James Version.

Edited by Lynn Copeland

Cover, page design, and production by Genesis Group (genesis-group.net)

Cover photo by Eddie Roman

Banana image: Nadiya Teslyuk © 123RF.com

"But I want you to know, brethren,
that the things which happened to me have actually
turned out for the furtherance of the gospel."
—PHILIPPIANS 1:12

To Allen Atzbi
(General Manager of Living Waters)

For years, whenever I needed anything or suggested
that something be done, Allen would simply email
back, "On it." And it would be done. Always.
"Who can find a faithful man?" (Proverbs 20:6).
I found one.

CONTENTS

INTRODUCTION

I t was early in March 2017. I had just spent twenty minutes pleading with a young lady who seriously wanted to commit suicide. I was interviewing her for an upcoming film on the subject of suicide and depression, and almost everything she said shocked me.

She even said that she would be forever resentful toward her parents for bringing her into this futile life.

When I asked Amanda about her beliefs in God, she told me that she was an atheist. God definitely didn't exist.

Because she was so strong in her convictions, after the interview ended I hesitatingly asked, "Do you know who I am?" When she said that she didn't, I meekly said, "Banana Man."

Her face immediately lit up and she exclaimed, "You're Ray Comfort!!! I went to a Halloween party last year as 'The Flying Spaghetti Monster,' and there was someone there dressed as you—Ray Comfort!"

Her words didn't surprise me. I knew how renowned Banana Man had become. His story is fascinating and one that I'm excited to share. This book looks behind the peel. I think it will encourage you and hopefully inspire you to be a little bolder in your faith, and to joyfully wear the mantle of humiliation that comes with being a biblical Christian.

CHAPTER 1

THE BANANA AND AMERICAN ATHEISTS, INC.

*"For a great and effective door has opened to me,
and there are many adversaries."*
—1 CORINTHIANS 16:9

W ould you have the courage to face me in a debate in front of 250 atheists at our national convention?"

These were the words of Ron Barrier, the national spokesperson for American Atheists, Inc.

It was February 2001. A week or so earlier, I had been sitting in my office when I had an idea. I had written a book on atheism, published a booklet called "The Atheist Test" that had sold close to a million copies, and spoken on the subject of atheism hundreds of times. I figured that might qualify me to speak to American Atheists, Inc. So I sent them an email stating the above and asking if they would consider me as a guest speaker, but leaving out the fact that I was a Christian author and preacher. My thought was that if God could open the Red Sea, He could easily open atheist doors.

They respectfully declined my offer.

But then I began getting emails from Ron Barrier. It was rather strange. He didn't want me to speak to atheists, but he wanted to start a dialogue with me. In retrospect, it was possibly God putting thoughts into his atheist mind. We emailed back and forth a few times before he suddenly challenged me to a debate at their annual convention in April. After I replied that I would *love* to debate him, and would even pay my own airfare from Los Angeles to Orlando, Ron said that it was on.

To ensure he had enough debate material, I sent him a copy of my book *God Doesn't Believe in Atheists*. A week later he pulled out of the debate. I presumed that he read the book. I was a little disappointed, because it looked like God didn't want me to speak at the American Atheists' National Convention after all.

OFF AND ON

I soon began to get emails from irate atheists when they learned that the debate had been canceled. One of them accused me of being a "chicken" for pulling out of the event, but I pointed out that it was Ron who deserved that title. A short time later, Ron issued the following statement (his capitalization):

> Without going into detail, the answer to the burning question on everyone's lips is, YES, I DID INITIALLY ASK HIM TO DEBATE AND, YES, I DID WITHDRAW

THE INVITATION AFTER I READ HIS IDIOT BOOK
"gOD DOESN'T BELIEVE IN ATHEISTS."

Apparently embarrassed by the incident, he renewed the debate offer and "sweetened the pot" by flying me to Orlando at their expense.

It was Friday the 13th, 2001. Good Friday. I had taken an associate with me, and as we entered our plush hotel room in Orlando, we noticed a generous gift basket with a welcome card. My associate picked up a bunch of grapes, popped one in his mouth and said, "Wow! And I didn't think atheists were such ni—" Suddenly he grabbed his throat, choked, and fell to the floor. (He was just kidding, of course.) The basket was a very nice gesture.

The next day, about forty Christians showed up from around the country, including a reporter, the publisher of *God Doesn't Believe in Atheists*, and a film crew from CrossTV. I was concerned that their permission to film the debate was a bit flimsy. All I had was an email from Ron Barrier that simply said, "I don't care what you do!"

When the crew quietly entered the convention hall to set up, a security guard asked them what they were doing. She turned out to be a Christian and said that she would be in prayer for the debate.

We then went into the atheists' bookstore where they kindly gave me a table on which I could place free copies of my book. While we were in the store, Ellen Johnson, then president of American Atheists, introduced herself and asked if the three large cameras in the convention hall were ours. When I said that they were, she replied, "Good. We will make sure we give you plenty of time to set up."

It was like a dream come true. Not only had I been given permission to fill their convention with Christian literature, but I would be presenting my case for God's existence to around 250 atheists, as well as filming it, and the debate—along with the gospel—would be broadcast live over their website.

It was like a dream come true... I would be presenting my case for God's existence to around 250 atheists.

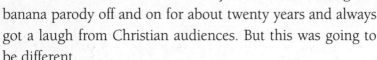

I was a little nervous because I was about to do a parody that made fun of atheism, and I wasn't sure if I could get my listeners to crack a smile. Atheists don't see atheism as worthy of being parodied, because they don't think it's ridiculous to believe that everything made itself. Christians think differently. I had been doing the banana parody off and on for about twenty years and always got a laugh from Christian audiences. But this was going to be different.

THE COKE-BANANA PARODY

I started by giving some statistics about Elvis impersonators in the United States. Here is the transcribed opening, from the "BC/AD" ("Barrier-Comfort Atheist Debate") recording:

> I would like to share, firstly, some life-changing statistics with you. So please listen carefully. According to an unofficial account, in 1960 there were 216 Elvis impersonators in the United States. In 1970, 2,400. In 1980 there were an estimated 6,300. In 1992, 14,000! Which

means by the year 2010, *one in four people in the US will be an Elvis impersonator.*[1]

Thankfully, they laughed. It was Bette Midler who said, "If somebody makes me laugh, I'm his slave for life." I didn't have 250 slaves for life, but I was thankful to be able to break the ice. So I picked up the Coke can and began:

> Millions of years ago there was a massive explosion in space. It was a big bang. No one knows what caused it, but from this bang issued a huge rock, and on the top of the rock formed a sweet, brown, bubbly substance. Then, over millions of years aluminum crept up the side of the bubbly substance and formed itself into a can, then a lid, and then a tab. Millions of years later, red paint and white paint fell from the sky and formed itself into the words "Coca-Cola, trademark, 12 fluid ounces."[2]

Then I said that anyone in his right mind knew that if the Coca-Cola can was made, there *must* be a maker. If it was designed, there *must* be a designer.

That's when I produced a banana and said,

> Behold, the atheist's nightmare. If you study a well-made banana, you'll find on the far side there are three ridges. On the close side, two ridges. If you get your hand ready to grip a banana, you'll find on the far side there are three grooves, on the close side, two grooves. The banana and the hand are perfectly made, one for the other.
>
> You'll find the Maker of the banana, Almighty God, has made it with a non-slip surface. It has outward indicators of inward contents: green, too early; yellow, just right; black, too late. If you go to the top of the

banana, you'll find, as with the Coca-Cola can, the makers have placed a tab at the top, so God has placed a tab at the top. When you pull the tab, the contents don't squirt in your face.

You'll find that the wrapper is biodegradable and has perforations, usually three or four. Notice how gracefully it sits over the human hand. Notice it has a point at the top for ease of entry. It's just the right shape for the human mouth. It's chewy, palatable, easy to digest, and it's even curved toward the face to make the whole process so much easier. That's if you get it the right way around.[3]

Some thought that it was funny. And they hadn't just cracked a few smiles. They *did* laugh, although not as enthusiastically as Christian audiences had so many times before. Of course, their laughter may have been cynical.

After a lively question-and-answer time, Ron Barrier came over and we shook hands. He even let me give him a hug. Some angry atheists came up to the platform and spat out a little sarcasm, while a number of others asked me to sign their books, which was unusual but kind of nice.

Andy Butcher, the reporter who attended the debate, published his account in a well-known Christian magazine:

Evangelist Ray Comfort stepped into the lion's den armed with a can of Coca-Cola and a banana...

Comfort's humor drew laughter and applause at first—but the reception got decidedly chillier as he went on to challenge evolution and atheism's foundations and when he quoted Scripture.

He produced a Coca-Cola can and presented his "theory" of how it came into existence—formed by chance over millions of years. To believe that was "to move into an intellect-free zone," he said, "to have brain liposuction." Then he pulled out from his jacket pocket what he called "the atheist's nightmare"—a banana.

Comfort said the banana, like the Coca-Cola can, had been cleverly designed for human use—and, unlike the can, was biodegradable...

Some members of the audience laughed and booed as Comfort spoke about sin and the need for salvation. In the question-and-answer sessions one man challenged Comfort to eat some strychnine-laced peanuts he offered, to prove the veracity of the gospel passage that claimed Jesus' followers would be able to drink poison and not be affected. Comfort declined, but said: "I know where I'm going if I do eat them."...

Later Comfort said that he had been grateful for the warm reception he had received. "Getting in there was no problem, it was getting out I was worried about," he laughed. "[But] they were very gracious. It was an opportunity to give God's Word uncompromisingly to some who usually wouldn't listen."[4]

I didn't know it then, but the reporter's observation that "Comfort's humor drew laughter and applause *at first*" would prove to be noteworthy some years later. Yes, God had graciously opened atheist doors to the gospel—and now the adversaries were about to come pouring in.

CHAPTER 2

THE NO-AUDIENCE TV VERSION

"For we have been made a spectacle to the world…"
—1 CORINTHIANS 4:9

It was a cool September morning in California in 2003. Actor Kirk Cameron and I were at beautiful Hume Lake, just north of Los Angeles. The air was still and crisp, perfect for filming an episode of "The Way of the Master." I couldn't have ordered anything better.

This was our television program's second season, and at that time it was airing in more than seventy countries. It had become very popular, not only because of its unique content, but because it was cohosted by Kirk, once known as "America's sweetheart." It is no exaggeration to say that he had been featured on the covers of heartthrob magazines almost weekly during most of the 1980s.

When a nationally known Bible teacher once asked me, "How did you get an *international* ministry?" I told him that it was easy. You simply have a wildly popular Hollywood actor call you and suggest combining his ministry with yours.[3]

When my wife, Sue, and I once had dinner at Kirk's parents' house, I saw old photos of Kirk as a teenager with President Ronald Reagan and with Lucille Ball. As a star of *Growing Pains*, Kirk was so popular that Lucille Ball came to his trailer on the set to meet him while they were both taping a TV special. Kirk was embarrassed to admit later that, at the time, he was just a seventeen-year-old kid and had no clue who she was.

I was extremely pleased that there was no wind as we were preparing to film at Hume Lake, because our backdrop for the program was the actual lake, and it looked like a mirror. It was picture perfect.

The episode we were filming was on the subject of atheism, and of all the arguments against atheism, one of the simplest and most logical is the teleological argument of design. Anyone with an intelligently designed and working brain can look at the beautiful design of nature and intuitively know that a Creator exists. Of course, atheists would disagree, but this is the teaching of the Bible and the result of common sense:

> For since the creation of the world His invisible attributes are clearly seen, being understood by the things that are made, even His eternal power and Godhead, so that they are without excuse. (Romans 1:20)

For more than twenty years prior to this day, I'd been teaching on the subject of atheism, and I had included the teaching in the script of the television program we were about to film.

KIRK'S WARNING

As a rule, I would write a script, Kirk would give his wisdom, then we would tweak it together. But this time I wanted to vary from the script a little. As Kirk was going over each page for the final time, I grabbed a Coke can from the film crew and went searching for a banana. We were filming at a camp, and I made my way to the kitchen in hopes of finding one. And I did. It wasn't perfect, but it would do the trick.

I had been using the routine with the Coke can and banana since the 1980s down-under in New Zealand, when I preached in the open air. As I did so I would often wear a T-shirt that read "I don't believe in atheists . . . see back," and on the back would be "The *fool* has said in his heart 'There is no God.'" After moving to the United States in 1989, I incorporated the routine into the opening of my standard teaching on atheism.

As we waited by Hume Lake for the production crew to adjust the lighting, I was aware that Kirk had never seen the routine. I had intentionally left it out of the script because I had done it so many times, thinking I could easily wing it without the aid of a teleprompter. Knowing he wasn't familiar with it, I quickly ran through it for his approval. We often made last-minute improvements to the script, and I was sure that he would love it.

But to my surprise he had serious misgivings, saying that atheists would mock me for it. I told him that I was used to being mocked; after many years of preaching in New Zealand, it was par for the course. Christians thought the routine was funny, and so did some of the atheists at their national convention. "The Atheist Test" booklet opened with the banana routine, and it had by then sold over a million copies. Besides, this program was intended for Christians, not for atheists.

Kirk was very gracious and didn't make a big deal of it. So we filmed it despite his misgivings, kept it in the finished program, and never gave it a second thought.

THE NEW YORK ATHEIST DEBATE

Fast forward a few years. Our "Way of the Master" TV program was now award-winning and airing in 170 countries. In 2007 I had talked Kirk into doing a televised debate with atheists. It took a bit of persuading on my part because he was so well-known in the secular world, and it was bound to attract secular media attention. I was often mocked for my faith, but Kirk had been America's sweetheart. Not just *America's* sweetheart, but reruns of *Growing Pains* in countries like China had made him extremely popular around the world. His appeal was a huge benefit for our program and its evangelistic success. Many times we heard of non-Christians channel-surfing and seeing "Mike Seaver" with a Bible. Kirk's sitcom character was a fast-talking, good-looking, likable teenage rebel, and he was the last person they expected to see with a Bible on his lap. So they beached themselves on a Christian network and stayed to hear the gospel. His involvement was a godsend for our show, and we didn't want to blow it by making unwise decisions.

One concern was that atheists had no reputation to lose, and so they might get angry in a deliberate attempt to draw media attention. There was a famous incident years earlier where a program that began as a cordial debate ended with chairs being thrown across the studio. It became big news. We didn't want that to happen, so we both agreed that we would be extremely gracious—*over-the-top, non-combatively gracious*. Our agenda was simply to proclaim the gospel and to do it with love and kindness.

We had planned to hold the debate in a well-known church in Hollywood. But as we were ironing out the details, one of the atheists pulled out. Then I found out about something called "The Blasphemy Challenge." On January 30, 2007, ABC News reported:

> Brian "Sapient" is an average-looking 30-year-old guy who works out of his basement in Philadelphia. His job? Well, Brian is taking on God.
>
> "Wow, that's a dramatic way of putting it," says Brian, who asked that "Nightline" not use his real last name for safety reasons. But however he defines his challenge, Brian is on the cutting edge of a new and emboldened wave of atheism.
>
> "There isn't any good reason to believe in God," asserts Brian. "It's that simple."
>
> What's wrong with God?
>
> "What's wrong with the tooth fairy?" asks Brian. "There's nothing wrong with something that most likely doesn't exist."
>
> There are an estimated 20 to 30 million atheists in the United States these days, and some of them say they feel like a persecuted minority.
>
> "Atheists are completely vilified. And it's OK," says Kelly, an atheist who works alongside Brian and also asked that her last name not be used.[6]

Brian and Kelly had the idea to publicize atheism by blaspheming the Holy Spirit publicly. The Bible labels it the unpardonable sin, and they didn't believe it; neither were they scared. It wasn't long before they had over eight hundred people who posted online video clips of themselves saying that they denied the Holy Spirit, thinking that was blaspheming the Holy Spirit.

Brian told ABC News that he was open to dialogue with Christians, saying, "If they want to come to the table and present their evidence, I will present my evidence. And we will see how much of theirs is based on faith, and how much of mine is based on fact."[7]

About a year earlier Kirk and I had done an interview with ABC *Nightline*, so we contacted them and suggested a debate about the existence of God. They were more than congenial. We then researched the likes and dislikes of Brian and Kelly, and purchased gifts for each of them.

However, there were a couple of problems. Brian was seriously fearful of flying, and he was also afraid of crowds —with a particular concern that a Christian crowd would turn violent. The second fear was unfounded, but we settled on a venue in New York that was within driving distance for him and Kelly. I also assured him that we would not invite thousands of Christians. The debate would be private, held in a small church building, and the audience would be limited to about one hundred people.

We allowed our opponents to bring fifty people, and instead of inviting our supporters to come to the debate, I simply asked the church in which we were filming to provide fifty people for the audience. That would prove to be a *big* mistake.

Then Kirk and I flew to New York.

Over the years of traveling together, it was very common for Kirk to be recognized and for airlines to freely upgrade us to business class because of his celebrity. Flight attendants would say that when they were teenagers they had his poster on their bedroom walls. I took advantage of this interest and would have him sign special gospel tracts that had his picture, to give to those who approached us. Kirk loved it because it gave purpose to his popularity. Instead of running *from* crowds, we ran *to* them for the gospel's sake.

On one occasion we were walking through the Chicago airport when I noticed a young lady sitting on the floor leaning against a wall. I walked over and gave her one of our Million Dollar Bill gospel tracts, and asked, "Have you heard of Kirk Cameron?" She said that she had. "Would you like to meet him?" She looked at me and gushed, "Oh, yes!" I called Kirk over, and they chatted for a few minutes, then he signed her Million Dollar Bill. As we walked away, I glanced back and saw her very sincerely mouth the words *Thank you!!*" I felt like Santa Claus on steroids. Meeting Kirk was something I was sure she'd never forget.

THE DEBATE

We arrived in the excitement of New York City. As we approached the destination, security quickly ushered us past a small crowd and into the back room of a traditional church building. There we met our atheist friends for the first time and gave them their gifts. We then went over the program with the moderator, and a little later we began filming.

To my surprise, the moderator allowed the audience to react with applause. Normally, after the initial introductions, the moderator would ask the audience to hold their applause, for obvious reasons. I presumed that would happen here. But it didn't. The result was that the fifty atheists were like delirious fans at a Super Bowl. Anytime a member of their team made any sort of point, as far as they were concerned, it was a winning touchdown. But anytime we said something, there was comparatively little audience reaction. This was probably because most of the audience members the church had provided were nice traditional church folks, who politely gave obligatory applause. I'm sure that they didn't have a clue who we were, despite Kirk's fame. The impression that a point had been scored every time the atheists spoke was powerfully convincing.

It would have been very discouraging, without the consolation that we had been faithful to the Great Commission.

There were two other factors that played against us.

The first was that the moderator was a well-known TV personality who had visited our facility in California a year or so earlier to interview us about our ministry. As we gave him a tour of the studio, he took us aside and confided that he was a Christian. He asked us not to announce that, saying that if it became widely publicized that he was a believer, it might compromise his very high-profile job.

However, when he opened the debate up for audience questions and I did my best to answer a question about why there is human suffering, he wouldn't let it go. He was on the edge of being antagonistic. I found it strange because I expected him to be unbiased.

A few years later he was fired from MSNBC for saying something filthy about a female conservative politician on live television.[8] It was then that his bias made sense.

Another element that played against us was our desire to avoid contention. What we didn't realize was that many Christians wanted to see a brutal war of words. It was a battle between two opposing worldviews; they understandably wanted to see the atheists put in their place, and what they had hoped to see didn't happen.

With the enthusiastic applause from the atheist audience, the antagonistic moderator, and our deliberate lack of a fighting attitude in battle, the general perception was that we had failed. Miserably.

So in the following days, few said, "Way to go, guys! You faithfully preached the gospel!" Instead, the Internet was alive not only with atheists mocking us, but with well-known Christians writing articles like "The Way of the Disaster." It would have been very discouraging, without the consolation that we had been faithful to the Great Commission.

But things were about to get worse.

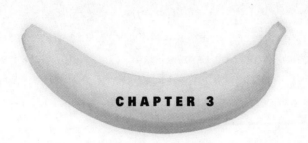

CHAPTER 3

THE BANANA CLIP

"I have become all things to all men,
that I might by all means save some.
Now this I do for the gospel's sake..."
—1 CORINTHIANS 9:22,23

A round that time someone mentioned to me that the banana clip was all over the Internet. I couldn't think why it would be. But I soon found out. An anonymous atheist had created his own YouTube video in which he captured the banana scene from our TV program and removed the Coca-Cola portion. That meant there was no longer a comparison between the two and it was no longer obvious it was a parody. He then argued that the banana didn't originally look like that. The popular yellow variety I had used was the result of thousands of years of domestication by humans, so it had nothing to do with God making it for mankind.

The clip was embarrassing, but it was just another bump in the road. It would soon be forgotten. So I thought.

But the YouTube clip went viral when Professor Richard Dawkins mockingly did my routine during a television interview and a number of times while addressing university students, calling me "The Banana Man." That suddenly spawned numerous spinoff videos of me wearing banana suits or holding bunches of bananas, and even Banana Man cartoon strips.

Professor Lawrence Krauss and other high-profile atheists used the clip in their university lectures as an example of the ultimate dumb creationist argument.

When I was in public strangers would yell, "Hey, Banana Man!" and run off laughing. I saw videos of hecklers yelling at open-air preachers down under in Australia, telling them that they sounded as dumb as "Banana Man."

When I was invited to do interviews on atheist radio programs, I had the impression they were taken aback when they heard that I could actually string whole sentences together. Atheists from around the country would show up with their cameras as I regularly preached in the open air at Huntington Beach in Southern California, trying to get me to say something crazy so their video would go viral.

Respected churches began questioning me, wanting to know if I *really* believed that the banana was proof of God's existence. Adding to the embarrassment was the fact that I had dragged Kirk into the circus with me. His wise words of warning came back to haunt me many times.

SOME WELCOME ADVICE

A few years later, my friend and preaching buddy Stuart Scott was driving with me to Huntington Beach, where we preached every Saturday for many years. "Scotty" was a wealth of wisdom. His understanding of science amazed me.

We would often talk about the wonders of creation and be in awe at the utter genius of the Creator.

During one of these drives, Scotty shared his thoughts about the Banana Man fiasco. He reminded me that it had given me an instant international profile among atheists. He was right, though it wasn't the sort of profile I enjoyed. I had become infamous in the atheist community.

Yet there was something strange about my infamy. *Atheists didn't feel threatened by Banana Man.* They invited me on their programs and let me talk about anything I wanted to talk about, and that included sharing the gospel with their atheist audiences. The "clown" could actually juggle words, and if he breathed a little fire, who cares? It was a kind of entertainment for them. After Scotty's encouragement, I began to see things from a different perspective.

And so I embarked on a strange and wonderful journey.

I started to notice that when I was on atheist programs, they typically garnered more than the normal attention— some receiving hundreds of thousands of YouTube views. When atheists reviewed our movies (such as "180" and "Evolution vs. God"),[9] they would get a massive audience. The original "Banana Man" clip[10] from our TV show quickly topped over a million views and inspired dozens of popular spinoffs.

I continued to be a curious object of atheist fascination. *How could any sane human being believe what I believed*—that the banana was actually made by God for man, when it had so evidently been genetically modified by man?

My blog became so inundated by atheists that I changed its name to the more fitting "Atheist Central." Thousands of skeptics faithfully frequented it and left so many comments (sometimes over a thousand on a post) that it was almost impossible to adequately moderate it.[11]

They stayed despite rules requiring that they respectfully capitalize "Jesus" and "God" and that they not mock or use bad language, or they would be banned. If I did ban someone, other atheists would plead for me to let the person back in. It was as though I had cut off a limb.

I tried to analyze why so many thousands of unbelievers would daily read and comment on a Christian site. When I asked why they kept coming back, some said that I was like a train wreck. They couldn't look away for a minute because they might miss something interesting:

> Really, Comfort's books and ideology can best be described as one massive train wreck. Except, instead of a train, we have his life.[12]

Others said that they were there to correct me for my unscientific remarks and for what they saw as misinformation about evolution. Whatever the case, it was Banana Man that brought them there, and for that I was grateful. Jesus said we are to be fishers of men (see Mark 1:17), and here the fish were jumping into the boat.

GOING BANANAS

The day after I interviewed outspoken atheist Professor "PZ" Myers for our movie "Evolution vs. God," he posted an entry on his blog with the headline "I met Ray Comfort tonight."[13] He included photos of us taken during the interview while two atheists used bananas to sword-fight in the foreground. Others created special Wiki pages about Banana Man.[14] There were also Banana Man videos in other languages, as well as mocking Banana Man songs and Banana Man posters.

When I was interviewed on "The Atheist Experience," a webcast and cable TV show, the hosts kept a banana in view for the entire one-hour interview. But they did allow me to share the gospel, and despite that, it became their most popular video, with over 500,000 views.[15]

Atheists found that they could increase interest in their YouTube videos by using my name in a derogatory way. If they called a video "Ray Comfort is Satan," it would generate thousands of views. Someone took one of our interviews of a woman in Hollywood, in which there was a clear gospel presentation, and renamed it "Ray Comfort Gets Destroyed." Our original clip had only 30,000 views but their version quickly received hundreds of thousands of views.[16]

A well-known atheist began reading my books out loud to other atheists, word for word—including the gospel messages.

A well-known atheist began reading my books out loud to other atheists, word for word—including the gospel messages. Then he would provide his own opposing commentary.[17]

Two nationally syndicated television programs from my home country of New Zealand requested interviews, and both sent camera crews to Southern California. One of them, *Sixty Minutes New Zealand*,[18] asked if they could bring up the subject of Banana Man, but at that time I didn't feel comfortable in that skin and didn't give them permission. Despite that, both programs painted the ministry in a very positive light.[19]

Atheism TV produced a low-budget series called "Banana Man & CrocoDuck Boy," based on Batman and Robin.[20] Someone wrote "The Banana Song."[21] When I spoke at churches, atheists would show up with a camera and request interviews. Some were very respectful and let me share the gospel, which they then posted online.[22] Others weren't so nice.

The Huffington Post "Religion" page had an article titled "Ray Comfort's 2006 Hysterical Banana Argument Demonstrates What Creationists Mean By 'Proof.'"[23] One artist, creating a series of sketches for YouTube, described drawing me in a superhero suit:

> Comfort would grab thin air manifesting a zipper, pull a banana peel around him and then emerge as Banana Man . . . a superhero coming out of a banana has got to be one of the strangest things I've drawn yet.[24]

To atheists, I had become the international celebrity-idiot poster-boy for creationism.

CHAPTER 4

PUTTING ON
THE CLOAK

"Humble yourselves in the sight of the Lord,
and He will lift you up."
—JAMES 4:10

In 2009, I was challenged to a debate by an atheist known as "Thunderf00t," atheism's biggest online video presence. (His YouTube channel has had over 150 *million* views.[25]) I ignored him at first, not knowing who he was among the thousands of atheists who frequented my blog. But for some reason he persisted, as though it was really important.

He wasn't the only high-profile atheist who wanted to debate me. It was a little weird, because I wasn't exactly an intellectual challenge. I was dumb old Banana Man—a no-name sheriff in a Western town who kept getting challenged by outlaws wanting a shoot out. I couldn't at that time see how "I buried Banana Man" was good for any atheist's reputation.

But, because he was polite, I decided to accept, and invited Thunderf00t to our ministry in Southern California.

A few weeks later, when I saw his car pull into our parking lot, I went out to meet the famous Thunderf00t. One would think that with a name like that he would have some sort of commanding presence. But he was just an unassuming and very likable English gentleman named Phil. Nothing about him thundered, or even echoed.

After some small talk, we each set up our own cameras in our studio and began talking for about an hour. Then Scotty and I took him to lunch.

When Phil posted the video on YouTube a few days later, it immediately received thousands of views, and then quickly moved to hundreds of thousands.[26]

In the comments section, I was, of course, vilified, mocked, and the object of hatred. However, I was surprised to see that he was crucified by atheists. They expected him to crush Banana Man under his thunderous foot, but in the courtroom of public opinion Thunderf00t slipped on appeal. The case was lost. They said that he looked weak and nervous, and someone even produced a cruel video of him, isolating his nervous stammering as he spoke with me.[27] It was very sad.

He was clearly wounded by the friendly fire, so much so that he made a special video in which he tried to justify what they saw as his poor performance. In his "Reflections" on our discussion,[28] he said that he had walked into the lion's den, that atheists "wanted to see blood" and he hadn't delivered. After the New York debate, I could empathize with him.

So about a year later he came back for another try, and again he stayed for lunch. This time his fellow atheists thought he fared better.[29]

OPENING DOORS

When I heard that the new president of American Atheists, Inc., David Silverman, was in Los Angeles, I decided to put on my Banana Man cloak and see if it would open doors.

I emailed him and asked if we could meet for lunch. To my surprise, he said that he would love that. So the president of our ministry, Emeal ("E.Z.") Zwayne, and I had a very congenial lunch with him. During the meal David said that back in 2001 when he was in his teens, he was in the audience as I spoke at their national convention in Orlando.

It was as though Banana Man really was the star of a twisted version of a "Super Hero" series. The analogy was appropriate. I'm a very ordinary believer who was given a special cloak of humiliation that supernaturally opened doors into the heart of the elite atheist community. The only "kryptonite" that could render Banana Man powerless was pride, and as long as I had to wear the cloak, I had very little of that left.

My pride is also kept at bay because I'm a klutz. I'm the clumsy kid who spilled his milk, but who still does it as an adult. My life is one disaster after another. I walk into walls, hurt myself, hurt other people, drop things, and knock items over. Anyone who is close to me will tell you that. I'm continually embarrassing myself, so I easily slip into the mantle of Banana Man.

Take a typical day in my life. I was refilling the water dish in our chicken coop when I spotted some spiderwebs high up on the coop, so I got rid of them with our powerful hose.

I suddenly heard a scream from the yard behind ours. I ran into our house and went upstairs so I could see over the high wall at the back of our yard. That's when I noticed a woman watering her lawn. So I quickly grabbed a dozen fresh eggs from our refrigerator as I ran back outside, took a ladder, climbed up and said, "Excuse me. I just squirted you by mistake!" She was holding her hose and I couldn't help thinking that this might be the beginning of a water fight, so I added, "Here are a dozen eggs as an apology!" She burst out laughing and said, "That's okay. Thank you!"

After my talk with Scotty, and after seeing what it could do, I resigned myself to wearing the Banana Man image without shame.

That day I discovered a new way to meet the neighbors.

It was 5:10 a.m. one morning, and I was pleased that Sue was still asleep. She'd had a tough previous day, plagued with a migraine. She needed all the sleep she could get. As I lay in the dark, I began to think about how I would like to interview the man who managed the Beatles' first tour to the United States. He was a Christian who lived in Northern California. I could take a train and interview people as I traveled up the state. But did trains travel that area? I quietly grabbed the iPad from beside my bed and did a quiet search in the dark. They did run trains! In fact there was a YouTube clip showing people on an actual train. How interesting. It was then that my finger—without conferring with my brain —touched "Play." My poor bewildered wife suddenly woke up to the sound of a very loud train coming through our bedroom.

I wrote an entire book on dumb things that people do, called *101 of the Dumbest Things People Have Done.* I'm the main character in the book. After reading it, two separate women sent Sue sympathy cards. I wonder why?

THE WAY UP

After my talk with Scotty, and after seeing what it could do, I resigned myself to wearing the Banana Man image without shame. This was also because I knew that humiliation before promotion is so often the way God deals with human beings. The way up is the way down first.

We see this in the life of Moses. In Acts 7:22 we read, "And Moses was learned in all the wisdom of the Egyptians, and was mighty in words and deeds." He was a great man with great ability, but it took forty years of humbly tending sheep to get Egypt out of Moses. God didn't need or want the wisdom of Egypt or Moses' mighty words and deeds. But after his long humiliation, *in due time* he was promoted. God opened up big seas for him (see Acts 7:35,36).

It was the same with Joseph. He was humiliated by the betrayal of his brothers, sold as a slave, then humbled further by being wrongfully accused of rape and thrown in prison as a sexual predator. All the while he was innocent. But *in due time* God opened prison doors that opened big doors to the throne of Egypt (see Genesis 41:14–41). The way up was the way down first.

Before he became a follower of Jesus Christ, the apostle Paul was a respected Pharisee. He had the prestige of being brought up at the feet of Gamaliel, the great teacher of the Law (see Acts 22:3). He described himself as a Hebrew, an Israelite, and a descendant of Abraham (see 2 Corinthians 11:22). In his letter to the Philippian church, he says he was a Pharisee of the tribe of Benjamin, a Hebrew of Hebrews. But on his coming to the Savior, he lost everything:

> Yet indeed I also count all things loss for the excellence of the knowledge of Christ Jesus my Lord, for whom I have suffered the loss of all things, and count them as rubbish, that I may gain Christ. (Philippians 3:8)

He was hated, beaten, flogged, mocked, stoned, called "a plague," and the "ringleader" of a "sect" (see 2 Corinthians 11:23–25; Acts 24:5). When the Jews wanted to kill him, his only way of escape was to hide like a common criminal in a basket and be lowered over a wall.

He was arrested and thrown into prison even though he was innocent. But God opened doors for him to preach to Felix the governor, King Agrippa, and Caesar in Rome, and then pen most of the New Testament. God humbled Paul, then used him *in due time* for His purposes.

But the ultimate humiliation is seen in the life of Jesus. The Bible says that, in Jesus, "God was manifest in the flesh" (1 Timothy 3:16), restricting Himself to time and space, hunger and thirst, pain and suffering. At the age of thirty-three, He gave Himself into the hands of evil men who humiliated Him through mockery, spat on Him, beat Him, and then crucified Him on the cross of a criminal. The Bible says,

> [He] made Himself of no reputation, taking the form of a bondservant, and coming in the likeness of men. And being found in appearance as a man, He humbled Himself and became obedient to the point of death, even the death of the cross. (Philippians 2:6–8)

Jesus humbled Himself. But look at what happened *because* of that humiliation:

Therefore God also has highly exalted Him and given Him the name which is above every name, that at the name of Jesus every knee should bow, of those in heaven, and of those on earth, and of those under the earth, and that every tongue should confess that Jesus Christ is Lord, to the glory of God the Father. (Philippians 2:9–11)

He took on the form of a slave, or "bondservant," and we are to do the same. The Bible admonishes us, "Let this mind be in you which was also in Christ Jesus" (v. 5). In "lowliness of mind" (v. 3), we are here to humbly serve this world for the sake of their salvation. The humiliating "Banana Man" moniker has taken me down, but then has given me unique access to do just that:

And whoever exalts himself will be humbled, and he who humbles himself will be exalted. (Matthew 23:12)

We are to be,

clothed with humility, for "God resists the proud, and gives grace to the humble." Therefore humble yourselves under the mighty hand of God, that He may exalt you *in due time*. (1 Peter 5:5,6, emphasis added)

The result of those who humble themselves under the mighty hand of God is that He may exalt them for His use *in due time*. Moses had to learn meekness before God used him *in due time*. Joseph had to feel the pains of affliction before the *due time* of his release, and the Bible tells us that "*in due time* Christ died for the ungodly" (Romans 5:6).

CHAPTER 5

WHAT HARM COULD COME?

"But as for you, you meant evil against me;
but God meant it for good..."
—GENESIS 50:20

I t was coming up on the 150th anniversary of the publication of Charles Darwin's *The Origin of Species*. The book was now in the public domain so that anyone could republish it. I decided to write an introductory section refuting the unscientific theory, include the gospel, have the book published, and give it away.

My vision was to distribute thousands of free copies to students at fifty of the top universities in the United States. It would be a logistical nightmare, but I was confident that we could find teams of Christians around the country who would be willing to help us. My advisory board loved the idea.

So did Kirk. He thought the concept was wonderful, and to my delight didn't have any hesitation in lending his name to the project. After all, what could possibly go wrong? We were *giving away* a free book at places of higher learning. Books are sacred in universities. The only time I could think of that books were hated was in Nazi Germany in the 1930s. University students piled them up and burned them—a dark omen of things to come in Germany.

E.Z. strongly urged me to read the entire book, which made sense. How could I write an introduction for *The Origin of Species* when I hadn't read it? So I began to read the famous book.

It was like crawling through a desert wearing a ball and chain. Every page was made of lead. I should have suspected that Darwin was long-winded when I learned he originally titled his book *On the Origin of Species by Means of Natural Selection, or the Preservation of Favoured Races in the Struggle for Life*. To say that it was dull, dry, dusty, and extremely boring would be a gross understatement. But I did eventually come staggering out of the desert.

To let our supporters know about the "*Origin* Into Schools Project," we released a short YouTube video with Kirk explaining the plan to give away 50,000 copies at the top universities in the country. We had no idea that the clip would soon kick a massive and nasty hornet's nest.

THE HORNET'S NEST

Videos vilifying us suddenly appeared everywhere online. One almost immediately received over a million views. The female atheist in the clip said in a thick French accent:

> In case you haven't heard about it, there's a very special publication of *The Origin of Species* that will be given

away free. And what I mean by "special" is that it's going to have a fifty-page introduction to it, written by yours truly, Ray Comfort, the banana guy.[30]

A wildly popular atheist program called "The Young Turks" responded with a video to their massive list of subscribers. They called it "Kirk Cameron's [expletive] Creationist Plot Against 'Origin of Species.'" They opened with, "Kirk Cameron has hatched a little plan with his friend the Banana Man," and went on to call it an "asinine plan." A mass of other videos appeared, accusing us of assaulting Darwin's book, with one calling it "The Retarded Edition." Even RogerEbert.com (site of the former movie reviewer) contained a piece titled "Kirk Cameron Combats Darwin in Bananaland."[31]

The National Center for Science Education (NCSE) not only announced the date of our planned outreach, but they listed the targeted campuses and offered free downloadable graphics so each university could print their own countermaterial.[32]

In an article entitled "Ray Comfort Is Bananas," the NCSE stated:

> Executive Director Eugenie Scott takes aim at creationist Ray Comfort's distorted views on evolution in a debate taking place on the *U.S. News & World Report* site. The debate centers on Comfort's 54-page introduction to a "special" edition of Darwin's *On the Origin of Species* that will be given away on college campuses across America starting November 19th.[33]

Dr. Scott urged students to take the free copy of *Origin* that we were offering, but to not "waste your time with the middle section of the introduction."

Professor PZ Myers wrote on his blog,

There is a strategy to address this obscenity. They're giving the books away for free: just get one or a few... [R]ip out the introduction and donate the rest of the book to charity... But anyway, let the intelligent, rational community sop up these sad mutilations of a great book and tuck them away from the gullible.[34]

The professor encouraged atheists to become the intellectual savior for all the dummies out there who can't think for themselves. The great masses in universities are such shallow thinkers that their copies need to be censored. My introduction had to be hidden from "the gullible."

When a university student at a lecture asked what Professor Richard Dawkins thought of the *Origin* giveaway, he told the student body:

Ray Comfort is a New Zealander living in the United States. You may know him as the Banana Man. Look him up on YouTube [laughter]...A lot of people seem to be very worried about this. I can't really get that excited about it. I mean, presumably people at universities are capable of seeing through that kind of thing. And, I imagine they would be rather glad to be handed a free copy of *The Origin of Species*. Just rip out 50 pages. And use the pages for the purpose they are best suited. And there you are. You've got a nice book.[35]

Atheist forums weren't so nice. They called for book burnings: "I'm not into burning books, but this one deserves to be," wrote one contributor. "Anyone up for a large bonfire?" Another warned, "Efforts at UC Berkeley will be met with unilateral resistance."

Our YouTube channel was filled with comments by angry atheists. One wrote,

> Seriously, I hate Ray Comfort now. I mean really hate him. He might try and sound polite, and sound like he's just trying to reason with you and that he really cares about you. In reality, he's just trying to make himself feel that he's right. He's also very disrespectful (in a respectful manner)... I hate Ray Comfort.[36]

Why were many atheists so angry? Why would they talk about book burnings, and threaten to resist the giveaway and rip out the introduction? There have been more than 140 different editions of Darwin's *Origin of Species*, many with special introductions. If atheists think my arguments have no merit, it doesn't make sense that they'd feel threatened by what I've written. Surely, if the introduction is ignorance and foolishness, intelligent students would see right through it.

CHANGE OF PLANS

"Common Sense Atheism" wrote about "Banana Man's" giveaway, revealing that they already had a thousand-member Facebook group focused on interfering with our distribution of *The Origin of Species*.[37] So with atheists planning to take as many books as possible and tear out the introduction, we decided to change our distribution date.

When Kirk and I showed up at UCLA with a large team and two thousand books, atheists approached us wide-eyed saying, "You're not supposed to be here today. *You're a day early!!!*" They complained that they didn't have their counter-materials printed and hadn't finalized plans for their protest. The Democratic Underground said,

> Ray Comfort is dropping his ID-ified *Origin of Species* bomb a day early. To counter the counterattack planned for tomorrow, his original ID-Day. Are there any DUers at universities where the Comfortites are out in force? Apparently, because people had plans to counter some of Ray Comfort's *Origin* giveaway—which was announced to occur on the 19th—Comfort is giving them away today. I've been getting reports from various universities that his minions are at work right now... Get out and grab yours now![38]

There was a buzz of Internet activity as atheists posted online videos and pictures of themselves holding up multiple books as trophies, and eBay was soon flooded with copies of the book for sale.

When Professor Dawkins originally told the university students to rip out the pages, he was very good-humored about it. But he wasn't too happy after around 170,000 copies were given out at a hundred universities, mostly unhindered. When asked on CNN about the giveaway, he was clearly angered. He suddenly had a problem remembering my name, and then he called me an idiot:

LONDON, ENGLAND (CNN)—A Christian evangelist branded an idiot by atheist biologist Richard Dawkins for trying to refute Charles Darwin's theory of evolution has brushed off the criticism.

Speaking to CNN on the 150th anniversary of the publication of Darwin's seminal work "On the Origin of Species," Dawkins said the evidence to support the theory that life on earth came about through natural selection, and not design by God, was "now massively buttressed by molecular evidence."

And referring to U.S.-based evangelist Ray Comfort, who argues that the universe and life is the result of an intelligent creator, Dawkins said: "There is no refutation of Darwinian evolution in existence. If a refutation ever were to come about, it would come from a scientist, and not an idiot."

"Hunches aren't interesting, hunches aren't valuable. What's important is scientific evidence. It doesn't matter what mister whatever his name is, Comfort . . . what his opinion is. It doesn't matter what my opinion is. What matters is evidence. And the evidence is clear. The evidence is in favor of evolution."[39]

We had originally planned to give away only 50,000 copies, but the venture was so exciting that Christians kindly gave to the cause and we eventually were able to give away a total of 200,000—in the United States, Canada, England, Australia, and New Zealand.

The "fame" of Banana Man helped launch the *Origin* project far beyond our expectations. By promoting the introduction, posted online, atheists unwittingly gave the gospel wings as its message of everlasting life reached an audience numbering in the millions.

We couldn't have done it without their help.

CHAPTER 6

MAKING SENSE OF THE "SENSELESS"

"But we preach Christ crucified, to the Jews a stumbling block and to the Greeks foolishness."
—1 CORINTHIANS 1:23

G eneral William Booth, founder of the Salvation Army, warned that the chief danger of the twentieth century would be a religion that offers Heaven without the warning of Hell.[40]

We saw that begin to happen in the twentieth century and it continues to this day. Many preachers avoid any mention of Hell, possibly because they have a concern that its existence paints God as a tyrant and them as unloving. Of course, atheists essentially deal with Hell by imagining that God doesn't exist. The rest of humanity, when pressed, have to admit that Hell is convenient for the likes of Hitler and a handful of other tyrants in history.

However, any mention of Hell has become comparatively rare in modern Christendom. The emphasis is typically on faith, relationships, success, prayer, prosperity, or prophecy.

Anything but warning that human beings are dying daily and will be damned for eternity in a terrible place called Hell.

Despite the fact that the Bible speaks of Hell more than it does of Heaven, for most in Christendom it's as though Hell didn't exist. This is why I was flabbergasted by a short video produced by Penn Jillette, the well-known magician of "Penn and Teller" fame and an outspoken atheist.

After a Christian gentleman had presented him with a Gideon Bible, Penn produced a brief video where he talked about how this man was loving, kind, and sincere. He then concluded with these amazing words:

> If you believe that there's a Heaven and Hell, and people could be going to Hell, or not getting eternal life, or whatever, and you think that, "Well, it's not really worth telling them this because it would make it socially awkward"... How much do you have to hate somebody to believe that everlasting life is possible and not tell them that? I mean, if I believed beyond a shadow of a doubt that a truck was coming at you, and you didn't believe it, and that truck was bearing down on you, there is a certain point where I tackle you—and this is more important than that.[41]

How could an atheist, of all people, have such profound and logical thoughts? Penn was eloquently saying what should have been blasted through church speakers at every pulpit on the face of the earth. This was very unexpected, and it was so refreshing that I wanted to contact Penn Jillette to personally thank him.

A friend of mine, Dean, was a talented magician who appeared multiple times on the iconic *Johnny Carson Show*.[42]

Someone had sent him another Penn Jillette video on You-Tube, where Penn spoke of intellectual people who believe the Bible (edited for language):

> And when they think that the Bible is the Word of God, I think they mean something else. I sometimes think that many other people are speaking in a code that I've not been given the key to. When someone says to me, "I believe in the Bible literally," well, I, personally, Penn Jillette, read about a chapter of the Bible a day. I just read through it, over and over again. So when someone says they believe in the Word of God literally, I go back and think about Genesis, where people are living to be nine hundred years old...And then I think about Noah and the flood, killing everybody? God that loves us kills everybody? And He wants to get two of every species, and seven of the ones that are clean, onto a boat that floats for that amount of time? And I just go, "*Really?* Because you don't act that way! You're able to go to Home Depot, you're able to pay with a credit card, you're able to go to Starbucks. You know how to use a computer. Really?"[43]

"How much do you have to hate somebody to believe that everlasting life is possible and not tell them that?"

Penn was clearly frustrated that intelligent people, who live like the rest of sane humanity—using credit cards and computers—*believe the craziness of the Bible!* The Noah flood particularly concerned him. As far as he knows there is no way that a man can make a boat to hold every kind of animal on earth, that people lived to nine hundred years, and that a loving God killed everyone. It makes no sense to him. A child could be excused for believing such unscientific foolishness, but not a rational, intelligent adult.

Then, instead of writing these people off as being insane, he humbly looks to his own shortcomings. *It is possible he was missing something?* Is there code of which he knows nothing? He continues:

> There's a code going on [for which] I need the Rosetta stone. I need someone to sit me down and go, 'Penn, when [the President] says he went to that church and they talked about all this stuff being literal, what he really meant was __.' Fill in the blank! Tell me! What does he really mean? These people are good, honest, smart, not crazy people, *so why are they saying crazy stuff to me?*[44]

Since Dean had a friendship with Penn, someone suggested that he try to arrange for the two of us to meet. When Dean asked if I would like to personally speak with Penn, if he could arrange it, I replied, "Dean, I would crawl over broken glass for ten miles to interview Penn on camera about the existence of God...It would be a heart's deepest desire for me to do this."

There *is* a key that Penn is missing to help the Bible "code" make sense. He wasn't interested in meeting with me, however. It looked as though God didn't want me to share the gospel with Penn Jillette.

AN ANGRY RICHARD DAWKINS

Penn isn't the only atheist astounded that otherwise intelligent people could believe the Bible is literally true.

It was a debate about Christianity, looking specifically at how Christians could believe the "silly" stories of the Bible. The moderator read a passage from the narrative of Lot (Genesis 19), turned to a Christian in the audience, and asked him if he believed that Lot's wife *really* turned into a pillar of salt.

You couldn't help but feel for the man as the camera pulled in close. He knew that he was about to look like a fool on national television. Despite the embarrassment, he said that he believed it literally happened because Jesus believed it.

In doing so, he was humbly bearing what the Bible calls "the reproach of Christ" (Hebrews 11:26).

Professor Richard Dawkins, in the same debate, was aghast that 45 percent of Americans believed in a literal Adam and Eve. Then he spoke of his disdain for the cross:

> Here we have a God who wanted to forgive mankind its sins including the sin of Adam...Why didn't He just forgive them? Why was it necessary to have a human sacrifice, to have His Son tortured and executed in order that the sins of mankind should be absolved? *Is that not the most disgusting idea you've ever heard?* Why didn't He just forgive the sins? Why did He have to sacrifice a scapegoat?[45]

Two thousand years ago, the Scriptures addressed this offense:

> And I, brethren, if I still preach circumcision, why do I still suffer persecution? Then the *offense* of the cross has ceased. (Galatians 5:11, emphasis added)

What Dawkins said later in the debate revealed why the cross was so offensive to him. He said that the criterion with which we look at passages in the Bible "is something that we all share—*it's that we are decent human beings.*"[46]

In other words, mankind is basically good. We don't need mercy or forgiveness. We don't require a scapegoat. What "sin" there is, is completely outweighed by all the good in man. The crime is so trivial, the judge can dismiss the case and all will be well.

Charles Spurgeon spoke about how the cross has no value for the person whose heart is steeped in pride:

> The philosopher puts his glasses to his eyes, looks at the Cross and then says, "I cannot see anything so very wonderful in it—even with these splendid glasses of mine, which can see more than that poor, humble peasant! I do not care about such a system of religion as that—any simpleton can understand the Cross." So he passes by and merely sneers at it.[47]

Then he addresses why there is such offense:

> And the Cross offends men, yet again, because it goes clean contrary to their ideas of human merit. There is not a soul in all the world that, by nature, loves to be stripped of all merit. No, the last thing a man likes to part with is his righteousness.[48]

When Dawkins says that we *all* share in decency, what does he mean? Is a rapist decent? Is a liar or a thief decent? Is a murderer? A pedophile? An adulterer? Who's to say who is decent and who isn't? And why is "decent" the criteria? The word simply means "conforming with generally accepted standards of respectable or moral behavior."

Does Richard Dawkins live by a generally accepted standard of respectable moral behavior? Some would say that he does, despite the fact that he thinks "mild" pedophilia is acceptable.[49] By today's standards it's more than acceptable that he has been divorced three times, and that he condones adultery:

> I want to raise another question that interests me. Why are we so obsessed with monogamous fidelity in the first place?...Why should you deny your loved one the pleasure of sexual encounters with others, if he or she is that way inclined? I, for one, feel drawn to the idea that there is something noble and virtuous in rising above nature in this way.[50]

He also thinks that it's morally okay to take the life of a human being in the womb, if the child doesn't come up to your intellectual standards:

> For what it's worth, my own choice would be to abort the Down fetus and, assuming you want a baby at all, try again. Given a free choice of having an early abortion or deliberately bringing a Down child into the world, I think the moral and sensible choice would be to abort.[51]

He refers to it as a "baby" and then says taking its life is a "moral" choice. Incredibly, he also believes that a baby in the womb is "less human" than an adult pig:

> With respect to those meanings of "human" that are relevant to the morality of abortion, any fetus is less human than an adult pig.[52]

Such is the "decency" of someone who believes that a human being, made in God's image, is nothing more than a species of animal among the beasts and is of no special worth.

On Judgment Day, God will not be judging humanity according to our accepted standards of behavior. We live in a society where it's generally acceptable to lie, blaspheme, fornicate, engage in homosexual acts, have an abortion, divorce, and view pornography.

Instead, God will judge us by the perfect righteousness of His moral Law (see Romans 2:12), and if the scales of eternal justice are not balanced on that Day, the Law will demand retribution. There will be Hell to pay.

In the cross of Christ, God was balancing the scales of eternal justice. The Judge came down from His bench to pay the fine for the guilty criminal. Just before Jesus died, He cried, "It is finished!" (John 19:30). In other words, He was saying, "The debt has been paid!"

But if atheism is true, then God doesn't exist and there is no divine Law, let alone retribution for its violation. Why pay a fine when no Law has been broken? It makes no sense. Christ dying on the cross seems ridiculous and barbaric. Again, the Bible puts it this way:

> For the message of the cross is foolishness to those who are perishing, but to us who are being saved it is the power of God. (1 Corinthians 1:18)

So it makes perfect sense that the gospel makes no sense to a proud, self-righteous atheist who believes that he's morally decent. The prodigal is covered in filth and thinks he is perfectly clean. He hasn't examined himself in the mirror of the Law.

Refusal to acknowledge our sins is rooted in stubborn pride. It fogs the mirror and self-deceives.

In reference to the prominent atheists of his day (back in 1898), Spurgeon said,

> Their efforts to oppose it [the gospel] are not worthy of our notice and we need not fear that they can stop the Truth of God! As well might a gnat think to quench the sun! Go, tiny insect, and do it, if you can! You will only burn your wings and die. As well might a fly think it could drink the ocean dry.[53]

We need not feel embarrassment or pity for the Christian who is scorned for believing God's Word. We know that Christianity is seen by the proud as being made up of "low-hanging fruit," uneducated dummies who haven't a scientific bone in their body. It is made up of idiots who are so illiterate and stupid that they have the audacity to believe that Noah built a ridiculous ark.

Instead, we are blessed who believe. God bless that dear brother who was willing to bear the scorn of the world on national television. He chose to trust in God and to esteem the reproach of Christ to be a greater treasure than the pleasures of this sinful world:

> By faith Moses, when he became of age, refused to be called the son of Pharaoh's daughter, choosing rather to suffer affliction with the people of God than to enjoy the passing pleasures of sin, *esteeming the reproach of Christ greater riches than the treasures in Egypt; for he looked to the reward.* (Hebrews 11:24–26, emphasis added)

MAKING EVERY PATH SMOOTH

The Bible says never to argue, but to be gentle and patient with the unsaved (see 2 Timothy 2:24–26). This is because they are spiritually blind; the god of this age has blinded the minds of those who don't believe (see 2 Corinthians 4:4). Just as we wouldn't put anything in front of a blind man that will cause him to stumble, we don't want to say anything that will cause sinners to stumble. We want to make a smooth path to the cross.

We are therefore discerning about what biblical truths we share in the gospel proclamation. This is because there are a number of things in the Scriptures that are hard for some to swallow. One of the hardest is Lot's wife turning into a pillar of salt. As Christians, we can easily believe that. We know that with God nothing is impossible. He can turn water into wine, raise the dead, open the Red Sea, walk on water, and multiply loaves and fish. We know that the miraculous is normality with Him. We also know that "God has chosen the foolish things of the world to put to shame the wise" (1 Corinthians 1:27).

The only reason the cross is foolishness to the lost is that it makes no sense when they don't see their sin.

So when I stand up to preach the gospel at a university, I don't say, "Hello, folks! I believe that God *literally* turned Lot's wife into a pillar of salt. Now let me talk to you about something important." My potential hearers don't have the faith that a believer has. Because their image of God is erroneous, they don't think about the fact that God has the ability to turn the whole universe into salt, if He so desired. Nor do they realize that it is more than compelling that Jesus believed it happened, or that God has chosen foolish things to shame the wise. To my potential hearers, I have said the equivalent of, "I believe in fairies; now let me talk to you about something important."

Instead, I want to sound reasonably sane so that they will listen to what I have to say. My agenda is therefore to try to present the gospel in a way that makes sense. The important point is, the only reason the cross is foolishness to the lost is that it makes no sense when they don't see their sin. It's not because *it is* foolish. It simply *appears* foolish to them—until they see their sin.

And so I want them to listen as I reason with them about "righteousness, self-control, and the judgment to come" as Paul did with Felix (Acts 24:25). While the governor listened to Paul's message, he trembled as it began to make sense. I therefore try to use "great plainness of speech" (2 Corinthians 3:12, KJV). If someone was in a house that was on fire and they didn't know it, I would keep my speech to them very simple. It wouldn't be a time to try to impress with eloquence. I want my listeners to understand that what I'm saying isn't rocket science—they are dying sinners and if they want to live, they need the Savior.

WHEN BOASTING SOUNDS GOOD

Boasting sounds good only to the boaster. To everyone else, it's nauseating. Scripture says, "Let another man praise you, and not your own mouth; a stranger, and not your own lips" (Proverbs 27:2). There are few things worse than someone winning a gold medal and then telling us how very good he was.

Dawkins was, of course, including himself when he said that we're all decent. In reality, we have a common descent with Adam and his sin. When a man denies that truth and instead thinks he's a primate, then he will beat his own little chest and boast of his goodness. He is king of his jungle. Such is the deception of self-righteousness. Lies told in eulogies rival only political promises before elections.

A great part of that deception is that despite the protests of Christians, the proud world believes that we live a good life to merit Heaven. If they would humbly listen to what we are saying and believe God's Word, the cross would make sense:

> For by grace you have been saved through faith, and that not of yourselves; it is the gift of God, not of works, lest anyone should boast. (Ephesians 2:8,9)

The only thing we can and should boast about is the sweet sound of the grace of God, and grace makes sense only when the Law has made a way for it.

CHAPTER 7

TAKING A RISK

"We are fools for Christ's sake..."
—1 CORINTHIANS 4:10

M y mind was preoccupied as I got out of the van after a long drive. I was fairly tired, but not as tired as I thought I would be after my five-hour flight from Los Angeles to Washington, DC. Then there was the drive through rain and heavy traffic, a radio interview in front of an audience, and about forty minutes of on-camera grilling by an atheist.

The atheist's name was Scott, a well-known filmmaker in atheist circles. He had been very polite in his emails as we previously worked out the details for the interview.

He was making a documentary about the 2016 Reason Rally, where 30,000 atheists were expected to gather on the Washington Mall, and we were in town to do an outreach there. The rally originally had quite a lineup of guest speakers, including Professor Richard Dawkins, Penn Jillette, Professor Lawrence Krauss, Bill Nye, actor Johnny Depp, and others. Unfortunately, Richard Dawkins had a stroke and was forced to cancel, and Johnny Depp had serious domestic issues, causing him to also withdraw.

Scott had told us his documentary was a big production where they were using ten cameras to get every angle, and he wanted to get my angle as a Christian. He was interviewing me to get "the other side" to make the documentary fair and balanced. I thought that attitude was very commendable and I was delighted to be part of it, even though I suspected he may depart from the questions he'd submitted beforehand. My attitude has always been to take a risk for the sake of the gospel. If someone wanted to make me look like a fool, I was willing to be a fool for the gospel's sake. Besides, how much more of a fool could Banana Man become?

GREAT SCOTT!

After entering a crowded hotel room around 9:00 p.m. on Friday, the night before the Reason Rally, I sat down for the interview. Scott sat beside a camera in front of me and asked questions.

To my surprise, he began by asking me about my conversion to Christ. I have learned never to hold back with atheists. This is because they almost always let me share the gospel, presumably because they consider it to be powerless. But it's not; it's the "power of God to salvation" (Romans 1:16). Every one of the millions who converted to Christianity have done so because they heard what the Bible calls "the everlasting gospel" (Revelation 14:6).

After some time, Scott asked me about the issue of slavery in the Bible, as well as other very important topics. Here is a portion of the transcript (published with permission):

SCOTT: What is faith? I loved your video where you talked about when you first had your awakening and it started from a fear of death. Did you start out with seeking evidence that this was true; say, this was true instead of the Quran or the Bhagavad Gita or the Book of Mormon? Or was it the fear that first made you make that leap of faith, or was it searching out evidence? Did you read all the sacred books and decide which one seemed more true?

RAY: The whole of humanity is in a helpless state in the face of this thing called death. Every minute a hundred people die, every hour six thousand, every day a hundred and fifty thousand, every year fifty-four million people like you and I die. And every one of them is crying, "*Oh, I love this life*." They've got a will to

My attitude has always been to take a risk for the sake of the gospel. If someone wanted to make me look like a fool, I was willing to be a fool for the gospel's sake.

live. We call it fear of death but it's a will to live, and it's God-given. We're human beings. We're aware of our existence.

And so at the age of twenty I wondered, why on earth won't people talk about death? We are all in this long line, people are stepping off a cliff, and I thought, *Can I get out of this line?* And so that night I just cried out, "Why?" I didn't even cry out to God. It was just, "Why?" Everything is futile if death comes at the end. It makes no sense. And then six months later, I was on a surfing trip. The gospel was explained to me, that we've sinned against God, we've violated

His Law; and like any judge proclaims a sentence, God proclaimed the death sentence upon the whole of humanity: "The soul who sins shall die."

That's why we die, and after this, the Judgment; and Hell awaits because God is just. But it also says God is rich in mercy and He provided a Savior. We broke God's Law, and Jesus paid the fine in full. Now, if we'll repent and trust in Him who died for us and rose again on the third day, God says He will remit your sins and grant you everlasting life as a free gift.

Hinduism doesn't offer forgiveness of sins, Buddhism, Islam. They're all works-righteous religions.

SCOTT: But how do you know that? I can see why this is a very comforting thought, but how do you know that it's true?

RAY: Let me explain it this way. All the religions are what's called works-righteousness religions. Hinduism, Buddhism, Islam, etc., say you have to *do* something to merit everlasting life. Christianity says you can't; you're a lawbreaker. Anything you offer God is an attempt to bribe Him to forgive your sins and grant you everlasting life. The only way we can be forgiven is if the Judge is merciful. And God is rich in mercy, and He'll forgive any sinner who comes to Him.

SCOTT: But how do you know that's true? Is it because of the logic of it? Why the faith in that? How do you know that Hinduism, that system, isn't true?

RAY: They can't forgive sins. There's no provision for forgiveness of sins in any of those religions; they're "works-righteousness." Christianity forgives us.

SCOTT: So it's more of a logic; you think that this could only be the way to God.

RAY: That's exactly right. You're up the river Niagara without a paddle. There's only one line being thrown to you and that's the line of the gospel, and God Himself provided it. Every other effort to save yourself is futile; you cannot save yourself. You can only be saved by God's grace.

SCOTT: So it just makes sense. It's more logical, that's why you believe that.

RAY: The gospel makes sense. But it only makes sense if you precede it with the Ten Commandments to show us we're sinners. When we realize we've lusted and lied and stolen, we're in big trouble, and God's provided a Savior so we can be forgiven. He paid the fine, so God could dismiss our case.

SCOTT: Can someone be moral without a belief in God?

RAY: Absolutely. What's the favorite atheist thing, "You can be good without God"? Yes. All you've got to do is choose your own standard of goodness. I interview a lot of people and almost everyone proclaims their own goodness: "I'm a good person."

SCOTT: What's your definition of good?

RAY: The dictionary has at least forty different definitions of "good." Number one is "moral excellence." That's my definition of good because I side with God's definition of good. "Good" means moral perfection in thought, word, and deed. If you talked to Adolf Hitler, I guarantee he would think he was a good person: "I cleaned up Germany, brought in full employment, got rid of brothels, cleaned up the scum, and purified the German nation."

A little girl was looking at a sheep eating green grass, and she thought how nice and white the sheep looked against the green grass. Then it began to snow, and the same girl looked at the same sheep and said, "What a dirty sheep, against the white snow." Same sheep, different background.

When you and I compare ourselves to the background of man, we come up reasonably clean. My life compared with Adolf Hitler's makes me seem like a really good person.

SCOTT: Right.

RAY: But on Judgment Day, God will judge us by the standard of moral perfection—absolute righteousness that considers lust to be adultery and hatred to be murder.

SCOTT: So it's kind of like a thought-crime?

RAY: Yes, absolutely. If you lust after a woman, you commit adultery in your heart. If you hate someone, God's knows if you had opportunity you'd probably [murder them] if you knew there was no punishment for your crime.

SCOTT: It almost sounds like George Orwell in *1984*, where they had thought-police and thought-crimes.

RAY: Well, let me qualify it. The average guy lusts after the woman next door. God knows, and he knows, if the woman said, "Come over, honey," he'd be over like greased lightning. The desire is the same as the deed in God's eyes.

SCOTT: Just having desire.

RAY: Oh, yes. The Bible says, "He who hates his brother is a murderer." That's how high God's standard is, and He sees our thought-life. He sees our motives.

SCOTT: Is it possible for anybody not to have this sort of thought-crime, this sort of lust at some point, when you see a woman walk by on the beach?

RAY: I've never met a guy who can say, "I've never lusted."

SCOTT: But doesn't that mean that God created us with this impossibility to live up to that standard then?

RAY: Well, none of us can. You could try that [defense] in a court of law. If you commit a serious crime and say, "Judge, I raped that woman, but God made me like this," that doesn't hold water in criminal court.

SCOTT: How could God hold you responsible for something that He put in you that you can't even resist? I mean it would be like an inventor inventing a toaster that then burnt the toast, and then blaming the toaster.

RAY: No, because the toaster's not a moral agent. You're a moral agent. You've got a conscience. Conscience means "with knowledge."

SCOTT: Right. But I mean if it's impossible for me to never have lust, then aren't you just setting me up for certain failure? I mean even though I could know it's wrong, I'm like, "But God made me that way."

RAY: Yes, but again, you can't use that in a court of law to justify yourself: "God made me like this, that's why I robbed the bank." "God made me like this, that's why I raped the woman." God holds us morally responsible, as do courts.

SCOTT: Right.

RAY: And so He's willing to forgive us and change our hearts if we'll repent and trust Christ. In an instant He'll do that. But if you continue in your sins, God will hold you accountable.

If I get to share biblical truths about how to find everlasting life with one person, I feel honored. This session was with fifty atheists for an entire hour!

SCOTT: So, are you able to then, once you repent, never have a lustful thought?

RAY: Oh, no. You battle it.

SCOTT: Oh, okay. So it's the trying not to do it more than the not doing it?

RAY: Well, there's a difference between "falling" into sin and "diving" into sin. The hypocrite dives into sin; he's playing the hypocrite. The Christian fights it, and if he falls into sin, he says, "God, please forgive me." He doesn't want to play the hypocrite. You will find the difference on Judgment Day, between the true and the false. Our churches are filled with hypocrites who dive into sin. They don't even fool us, and they won't fool God on Judgment Day.

NO PIZZA REQUIRED

Scott's attitude amazed me. He was asking all the hard questions that atheists asked, but he was politely saying "Right," to most of my answers, almost as though he was conceding to my points. It was such a contrast to the ABC moderator in the New York debate. It was a dream come true to be asked these questions and not be talked over or have to contend with rabbit trails.

I expected Scott to edit my answers on the final video, but he didn't. A few weeks after the interview he posted the entire conversation online.[54] *Nothing was removed.* Within three months the video had received over 100,000 views, and most viewers were no doubt atheists, because this was produced by atheists and promoted almost exclusively in atheist circles.

Let me see if I can put this into perspective. I was once speaking at a creation museum in Santee, California. After I spoke, I went to greet about fifty atheists who were protesting outside on the sidewalk. They were very friendly and it seemed that all of them were familiar with the Banana Man fiasco. So when I asked if they would like to get out of the heat into an air-conditioned room for free pizza, they all jumped at the suggestion. I told them that I wanted to film a question-and-answer session with them. No one objected, and so for the next hour I had a Q-and-A session with fifty atheists.

If I get to share biblical truths about how to find everlasting life with one person, I feel honored. This session was with fifty atheists for an entire hour! It was a wonderful opportunity to reason with them about their eternity.[55]

Nothing they said was new, except for one question near the end. The question was a good reminder that there was some "kryptonite" in the room. One polite atheist stated that the Bible clearly contradicted itself by saying that Judas purchased a field (Acts 1:18), but in another place it says that the religious leaders purchased it (Matthew 27:6,7). While there are many incidents in the Old Testament that I couldn't speak to with much expertise, I did know that it was the religious leaders who purchased the field. This is because Judas was dead at the time, and dead men don't buy fields.

So with an almost arrogant assurance, I told the polite young man that it was the religious leaders who had purchased it. To back it up, I said that I would give him one hundred dollars cash if the Bible said that Judas had purchased the field.

With cameras rolling, we got a Bible and he read it to me. Here are the passages that address the seeming contradiction:

> Then he threw down the pieces of silver in the temple and departed, and went and hanged himself. But the chief priests took the silver pieces and said, "It is not lawful to put them into the treasury, because they are the price of blood." And they consulted together and bought with them the potter's field, to bury strangers in. Therefore that field has been called the Field of Blood to this day. Then was fulfilled what was spoken by Jeremiah the prophet, saying, "And they took the thirty pieces of silver, the value of Him who was priced, whom they of the children of Israel priced, and gave them for the potter's field, as the LORD directed me." (Matthew 27:5–10)

> *Now this man purchased a field with the wages of iniquity;* and falling headlong, he burst open in the middle and all his entrails gushed out. (Acts 1:18, emphasis added)

The Bible does say that Judas purchased the field, so the atheist had a hundred dollars in his hands a few minutes later. But even though he was right, it was only a *seeming* contradiction.

The religious leaders had purchased the field *in Judas's name*, using the money he had returned to them. Items such as expensive paintings are often purchased by proxy. The dictionary defines "proxy" as the "power or authority that is given to allow a person to act for someone else." The person bidding for a painting is said to buy the painting, but he actually buys it in the name of (on behalf of) someone else who may not be present at the auction.

There are other examples of this in Scripture; for example, in John 19:1 we read, "So then Pilate took Jesus and scourged Him." But we know that Pilate didn't personally scourge Jesus; his soldiers did it in his name.

This incident was humbling, but it was a good lesson for me. I was consoled in the fact that we don't need to know the whole Bible before we share the gospel with others.

One of the greatest hindrances to Christians sharing their faith is the fear that they may not have a right answer or that someone may bring up a Bible passage that they can't explain. In such a case it's good to remember that the person with an experience is not at the mercy of someone with an argument. We are called to testify to the gospel. That's our commission. It's not our job to give an intellectual theological exegesis of the Scriptures to unbelievers.

If someone brings up a question that I find difficult, I simply say that I don't know the answer, but that I will try to find out if they really want to know. Sometimes the humility of acknowledging that we are not know-it-alls can speak to someone more than an eloquent answer.

Still, I was honored that these atheists let me speak to them. How often does that happen? Yet here was Scott asking me questions in a relaxed and congenial manner. This interview wasn't costing me anything. I didn't have to provide pizza. I didn't have to contend. Neither did we have to film it, edit it, and worry about promotion or distribution. Atheists were carrying that burden, and in future years it would perhaps be seen by hundreds of thousands.

I was honored to be a part of this because I knew that it was unusual. What seemed like curve-ball questions were softballs that brought biblical truths to the ears of those who might never darken the doors of a church. I quietly wondered whether God was speaking to Scott, and if he was secretly searching for the truth. Little did I know that we would clash big time via email sometime after this interview.

Because we never know how God is working in someone's life, don't ever be afraid to take the risk in speaking to people.

CHAPTER 8

THE BANANA MAN INTERVIEW

*"And we know that all things work together for good
to those who love God, to those who are the called
according to His purpose."*
—ROMANS 8:28

N ear the end of my interview with Scott, someone announced, "Lawrence Krauss is ready!"

These were sweet words to my ears. My interview with
Lawrence Krauss was going to take place! I was pleased because we planned to include it in our documentary "The
Atheist Delusion."[56] We were almost finished with production, so the timing was perfect.

I wanted to ask him the same four questions I had asked
a number of university and college students in the documentary. That line of questioning concluded with one scientific question that had turned them from staunch atheists to
believers in God, in a matter of minutes. I wanted to get his
reaction to that one question.

Having Professor Krauss in the film would also be a huge drawing card for atheists. They loved him. Besides, a favorite argument atheists had about our films was that I only interviewed dummies—despite interviewing four scientists, including PZ Myers and other professors from UCLA and USC, in "Evolution vs. God." But even if what Lawrence Krauss said was negative, his inclusion in "The Atheist Delusion" would be frosting on what was an already sweet cake.

I also didn't mind the conditions that he placed on me: I could ask only four questions, and we had to use the entire interview in our film or nothing at all. I was more than happy with that, but I requested that he confine his answers to about thirty seconds. My desire with the documentary (as with everything else) is to see the lost saved from a very real Hell. And to accomplish that, we wanted the video to be fast-moving to keep the viewers' attention.

Lawrence was aware that all the speakers at the Reason Rally had been warned not to be interviewed by me. The atheists were concerned that we would edit any interview to make them look bad, but this was an unfair accusation as we always edited with integrity. I admired Lawrence Krauss for not caring about what other atheists thought and agreeing to do the interview. He was comfortable in his own skin, was very outspoken, and had become internationally well-known—perhaps partly because Richard Dawkins continually spoke well of him.

It was getting late and so we had to wrap up the interview with Scott, break down the set, and drive to another hotel to film the interview with Lawrence. I didn't want to exhaust his patience and have him suddenly change his mind.

KRAUSS AND COMPANY

It was a Friday night with lots of traffic, and the sidewalk in front of the hotel was busy with people going in and out. My mind was filled with thoughts about meeting the professor. Would he be cold and indifferent, or even antagonistic?

Suddenly, my thoughts were broken by someone saying my name—a very warm and friendly Lawrence Krauss, walking toward me on the sidewalk. I was expecting to go into a hotel room, make a polite acquaintance, and sit down for an interview. Yet here he was, walking up to me like a long-lost friend. In meeting the notorious Banana Man, the celebrity of atheism, he was like an excited child finally coming face-to-face with Goofy at Disneyland.

We hugged, and then to my great surprise he said, "I'd like you to meet my friend, Penn Jillette." *Penn Jillette! What was he doing there?* I shook hands with Penn because he was so tall a hug would have only reached his knees.

It was then Disney photo time. The professor asked for a picture of the two of us, while Penn readied his phone and eagerly waited his turn. I knew what they were doing but I didn't mind. By now I was feeling comfortable in my own peel.

Little did Penn Jillette know that meeting him was very special for me. I had a sense that something was being divinely orchestrated.

The interview itself was to be filmed in Lawrence's hotel room. As we entered, four film crews were packed into the rather small space, each with their own set of lights, cameras, and sound equipment. That many camera crews added to the sense of excitement.

While Lawrence and I stood in the crowded room, he welcomed Penn and another celebrity as they came through the door. Penn was friends with stand-up comedian and actor Paul Provenza, who had been the Master of Ceremonies at the 2012 Reason Rally.

As Penn explained later on his podcast, Lawrence had told him that he'd agreed to be interviewed by me and asked if Penn wanted to come up to the hotel room and watch. Penn replied, "Oh, do I!? (Laughter) Boy, do I want to go up and watch!"[57]

When we sat down, Professor Krauss made reference to a canvas tote on the couch on which were printed the words "Imagine No Religion." He said, "John Lennon wrote that." I nodded and added that in his 1980 interview with *Playboy* magazine, Lennon talked about why he had written the famous lyrics.[58] Most atheists think of his song "Imagine" as an atheist anthem, not knowing that John actually considered it a type of prayer. It was doubly strange that they liked the phrase "Imagine there's no Heaven," because it's asserting that Heaven exists, and we have to *imagine* that it doesn't.

OPENED DOORS

The interview with Lawrence Krauss went well. I asked him the four questions, but he apparently had a lot on his mind and forgot to confine his answers to thirty seconds. I reminded him later about our agreement to keep it short, and fortunately, he allowed us to edit his lengthy answers for brevity in our documentary.

The ending of the interview was anticlimactic. There was no swordplay because I had agreed to sit and listen while he gave his answers. After about ten minutes it was all over, and here we were with four cameras rolling. Penn was standing behind one of the cameras and called out, "More!" That's when someone suggested that the professor interview me.

So, with the cameras still rolling, Professor Krauss interviewed me. Naturally, he asked about Banana Man: "I've always been fascinated by the banana interview you did, which I've shown in several of my lectures, and I know that it's very good of you to live it down. But are you embarrassed by that?"

I admitted that I was, very, but that it had (eventually) turned out for good.

When the original Banana Man video came out, it seemed that the whole atheist world suddenly became experts in explaining how bananas had been modified. The website "Raw Story" said:

> They [Ray and Kirk] couldn't have picked a worse example, because the bananas they were eating—the same kind you find at the store—are dramatically different from the wild bananas that humans first discovered. The banana as we know it, like many fruits and vegetables, was dramatically changed over time through the very selection process described by Darwin. Human beings were the natural force that induced the selection, tossing out bananas we didn't like and growing only the ones closer to the goal, until we got the banana we have now. Wild bananas and the bananas they claim god created look very different indeed.[59]

While the particular banana variety I used may have been genetically altered by man, that doesn't escape the fact that even the original, or wild, banana (whatever shape it may have been) was created by God. He graciously provided all foods for His creatures to eat, and He endowed everything He created with tremendous genetic variety to survive in various environments. He not only gave us delicious foods for our enjoyment, but He enables us to even breed new varieties.

Our interview concluded:

RAY: . . . It's been embarrassing, but it's opened huge doors for me. I've gotten to talk to atheists on radio programs, television programs, because of that.

LAWRENCE: Well, it's true, it opened the doors. I wouldn't have known who you were if I hadn't seen the banana thing.

RAY: Yes, so it's been great!

LAWRENCE: And so it's been good that way. Well, I hope it's been very good for you, and I really wish we did have a banana here for you to sign. But another time. Thanks again.

RAY: Thank you.

CHAPTER 9

FACING BULLIES

"But before all these things, they will lay their hands
on you and persecute you . . . But it will turn out for
you as an occasion for testimony."
—LUKE 21:12,13

After the interview with Professor Krauss, I remained seated on the couch and looked at Penn Jillette as he stood alongside one of the camera crews. *Of all the times I could speak with him, now was the opportune time.* The lights were still on and the cameras were still rolling. It *had* to be divinely orchestrated. I remembered how I had said I would crawl over broken glass to share the gospel with Penn. It was the perfect setting. But, much to my disappointment, he politely declined.

Clearly, it wasn't God's will for me to share the gospel with Penn Jillette.

Suddenly Lawrence became very thoughtful and said that he wanted to ask me something. Then he said, "No, it's okay."

I said, "Go on. I'm thick-skinned—like a banana."

"No, no," he replied. "You wouldn't have done this if you weren't."

I liked Lawrence Krauss. He was respectful and kind, and his comment about me showing up solved a mystery for me about why so many atheists wanted to debate me when I was such easy pickings. Banana Man wasn't an intellectual challenge for an atheist, and yet they wanted to engage me. It didn't make sense.

I finally figured out what was happening. It was the school-bully mentality. I was the little kid with glasses; they were like the popular big kid in school, the bully who thinks it makes him look good to grab the weakling's favorite book, throw it on the ground, and grind his foot into it. That would impress his peers.

One atheist "bully" got over 100,000 views on a YouTube video that showed nothing but dumb clips of Banana Man, ending up with him and his buddy saying they could beat me up verbally, even if they were half drunk.[60]

Like many others, I was bullied as a kid. I was a little nobody that big kids picked on to make themselves feel good.

When I was about nine years old, my friend Trevor for some reason challenged me to a fight. The bully, Digby, was standing over his shoulder at the time so Trevor was pretty bold. Digby chimed in and named the time and place for us to fight: four o'clock on the Tovey Street sand hill, by the beach.

When I showed up alone, Trevor, Digby, and his gang were waiting for me, and as the fight began something strange happened. *Digby stopped us.* He was blown away that I had showed up alone, and from that time on we all became friends.

I found that just showing up alone as Banana Man to do interviews often got the bully and the gang's respect. They may not like what I stood for, but it earned me a right to be their friend. And for me, that was huge.

Lawrence wanted to know why I kept doing the God-thing when it seemed so obviously senseless and anti-science to him. He could see that I was reasonably sane. It just didn't make sense.

LAWRENCE: I was going to ask why you persist. Are you trying to save people?

RAY: I can't save a soul.

LAWRENCE: Okay. Is it that you just feel you're called to do it?

RAY: I believe in the existence of Hell. I believe it's a very real place. With every ounce of sincerity and earnestness I've got, I want to warn people that God is just and holy.

LAWRENCE: And loving?

RAY: Oh, yes.

LAWRENCE: That's why He condemns people to eternity for torture. Because He loves them so much.

RAY: No. He will have His Day of Justice, when Nazis will be punished for their wickedness. But He is so thorough that He will punish lying and stealing, adultery and fornication.

LAWRENCE: *Forever.*

RAY: Yes. Time will be withdrawn.

LAWRENCE: That's a loving God. That's amazing—Saddam Hussein in the sky.

RAY: Fifty-four million people will die in the next twelve months, worldwide. I've found everlasting life; I'm totally convinced of that, and I just want to share it with other people. And all I want them to do is listen.

LAWRENCE: Okay. The other thing is, everlasting life to me seems like the worst torture.

RAY: It may be to you, but not to me, because it's a new world coming.

LAWRENCE: Can you imagine an eternity where you have to talk to me?

RAY: I would *love* that. I would be honored.

LAWRENCE: Thank you, and good luck. And God bless. Oh, I forgot to say the one thing I was going to say at the very beginning. Which was, it was very "Christian" of me to do the interview.

I found it very interesting that the professor, despite all the vilification of Christians by atheists, still considered the word "Christian" to be synonymous with "kind." Above all, Christians should certainly be known for our kindness.

LIVING FOREVER

It was also interesting that Lawrence said he couldn't stand the thought of living forever, and in one sense I can understand why. Of course, we have the joys of love and laughter, friends, family, and fellowship, the blessing of seeing our children grow, the blueness of the sky, sunrises and sunsets, the songs of birds, the pleasures and power of procreation, along with amazing music, overseas travel, exciting sports, great movies, mouth-watering food, and thirst-quenching drinks. There are limitless pleasures in life, and so much to do. It truly is wonderful.

But all the while it's a battle to hold on to what happiness we have. We watch unending news of massive floods, fearful fires, dreadful droughts, runaway national debt, horrific hurricanes, killer tornadoes, crushing earthquakes, poisonous pollution, societal corruption, senseless shootings, family members killing each other, kids starving overseas, rape, violence, terrorism, race riots, and people targeting police.

There is a *daily* dose of death and destruction, suicides and suffering, financial worries for those who have money, poverty for those who don't, tragic car accidents, health issues, termites destroying the foundation, gophers ruining the lawn, snails eating garden vegetables, fleas on the dog, ants invading the house, mold in the shower, rising prices, aging parents, the fear of cancer and a host of other terrible diseases like AIDS, heart disease, strokes, Parkinson's, and the nightmare of Alzheimer's.

There are the continual annoyances of debilitating headaches, excruciating back pain, canker sores, earaches, bladder infections, insomnia, horrible allergies, fighting traffic, as well as fighting to stay fit, the headache of identity theft, cyber theft, home burglaries, and the cost of security to keep the hands of thieves off your property.

People get mauled by dogs, bitten by snakes, eaten by sharks, diseased by mosquitoes, mugged by thieves, ripped off by con men, raped by perverts, or molested by pedophiles.

If that's not enough, as time passes the hair falls out, eyebrows turn into tumbleweeds, brain cells die, joints weaken, muscles wither, eyes fade, ears become fifty times bigger, so does the nose, the body shrivels, soft skin turns to leather, and ear hair reaches out to the doorposts.

Yet for the atheist, *nothing* is wrong. Life has no rhyme or reason, no plan or purpose, and offers no hope or help. It's just unfolding according to the mindless and cruel evolutionary process. It's survival of the fittest, and none of us are fit to survive, because nothing survives but death. After death takes you, it will move on to another unfit human being and kill him, at the rate of fifty-four million human beings per year. Too bad. It all seemed so promising.

On top of all that, the atheist has the gamble that he may be wrong with his insane idea that *nothing made everything* and Hell doesn't exist. In reality, it's no gamble. He can't win. He's playing Russian roulette with a fully loaded gun. In the meanwhile, his pride keeps him secretly living with a dread of death, until it puts an end (so he believes) to the misery of this meaningless life.

And who would want all *that* for eternity? What Lawrence said made sense, for his hopeless worldview.

But as Christians, we know that we live in a *fallen* creation. We know why all these things happen, and we have an immutable promise from God that an unspeakably wonderful new world is coming. We will inherit the earth without the Genesis curse. We will be given new bodies that won't age or become diseased. Those who think this sounds too good to be true need to soften their sinful heart and believe it. God can be trusted; He *cannot* lie. Their lack of trust in Him means they think He's a liar, which is very foolish:

He who believes in the Son of God has the witness in himself; he who does not believe God has made Him a liar, because he has not believed the testimony that God has given of His Son. (1 John 5:10)

When skeptics repent and put their faith in Jesus, God will confirm His promise to them through the new birth. They will have the "witness" within themselves. The first step is simply to believe His Word.

I smiled and said, "Now, you know 'goodbye' comes from 'God be with ye.' I just thought I'd tell you that."

After talking with Lawrence for a few minutes, I tried once again to convince Penn to speak with me. I didn't want to let this opportunity go. It was too good to be true. Penn was standing behind a camera, the lights were still set, and four cameras were rolling. All that needed to happen was for him to come in front of the cameras, and sit with me and chat. But once again he declined.

A MEMORABLE GOODBYE

As I was leaving the hotel room, Lawrence and I shook hands and he said a polite, "Goodbye."

I smiled and said, "Now, you know 'goodbye' comes from 'God be with ye.' I just thought I'd tell you that."

He looked at me with unbelief, and Penn said, "I'm not sure that's true."

"God be with ye. It's in the dictionary," I said.

Penn replied, "Not in the Oxford English."

"It is. It's in the Oxford English."

"I don't think so," Penn insisted.

Lawrence jumped in, "Hold on. Hold on, we have Google here. We can settle this."

Someone said, "A lot of science is determined by Google," as Penn added, "*All*."

"But you can't believe everything you read in Google. And if you're right, I won't believe it," Lawrence joked.

Suddenly everyone was looking it up online. A moment later, Lawrence read,

> *Goodbye* etymology. Oh, hold on. Hold on! "Late 16th century contraction of *God be with ye*."

"Well, you win this one," Lawrence said. "And the point is, I'm happy to admit when I'm wrong."

Someone else added, "We can all learn something here tonight!"

We all laughed, and as I left I said, "Nice to meet you guys!" And it certainly was.

I'm both honored and delighted when any unbeliever listens to anything I share about the Bible. When we share its message, we are sharing the words of eternal life. God has entrusted us with the most precious of seeds, and when there's an open ear, there's a possibility that the seed may find root in the soil of the heart. In the light of such thoughts, may God help us to see every Saul of Tarsus as an apostle Paul, and every bully as an eternal friend in Christ.

CHAPTER 10

PENN JILLETTE

"Delight yourself also in the Lord, and He shall
give you the desires of your heart."
—PSALM 37:4

About five minutes after my interview with Lawrence Krauss, I was standing with our production crew on the sidewalk outside the hotel. We were about to leave when I was approached by Penn Jillette and Paul Provenza. As a conversation began, our camera crew took the initiative and began filming.

Both Penn and Paul had some questions about the banana routine. They had an inordinate curiosity about it and kept asking me why it was funny. Again, atheists don't see atheism as qualifying for parody. They consider themselves intellectually superior to anyone who believes in the existence of God. As much as they protest the accusation, they believe in the insanity that nothing created everything. As the Scriptures say, "Professing to be wise, they became fools" (Romans 1:22). Atheists are fools who think they are wise. And so Christians laughing at atheism doesn't make sense to them. Why should anyone laugh at the thought that the universe could make itself? They believe it's possible that matter came from nowhere, it exploded without a catalyst, and the explosion created intricate order and amazing design. They think inanimate matter sprang to life and frogs eventually became princes. Nothing exploded into everything, with no cause, rhyme, or reason.

For the next thirty minutes we talked about the existence of God, who made God, the existence of the soul, and other interesting topics.

While my mind was occupied with the conversation, I was bubbling with a sense of excitement at what was taking place. I was conducting a conversation that I believed was divinely orchestrated, and I didn't have to crawl over broken glass for ten miles for it to happen. I didn't plan this, and yet it was occurring.

I was bubbling with a sense of excitement . . . I was conducting a conversation that I believed was divinely orchestrated.

What's more, both Penn and Paul were very respectful and polite.

When Penn asked who made God, I told him, as I had explained to Scott earlier that night, that God has no beginning or end; He's eternal. He exists outside the dimension of time that He created and then subjected us to. Then we talked about how the words "soul" and "life" are synonymous in Scripture.

Atheists normally dislike any thought of human beings having a soul. This is probably because the soul is closely tied to the spiritual realm, and they don't believe there is any such thing. The soul is invisible, and for most atheists, anything that can't be seen is discounted. One of their favorite taunts is that Christians believe in an "invisible sky daddy."

Yet we are surrounded by the invisible. Air is invisible. So are gravity, the wind, and love. History is invisible, as are television waves, energy, and radio waves. Of course, we believe in these invisible things because we can test or experience them, or because their existence is just a matter of common sense.

A builder may not be visible because he is dead, but we know he was a reality because the building exists. The same applies with a painter. We don't say that the *Mona Lisa* had no painter simply because we can't see him.

We can experience love, experiment with the wind, and measure things like radio and television waves. History is just a matter of common sense, and I would argue the same when it comes to the existence of the soul.

For example, Penn Jillette is six foot six in height. We know he was small as a child, but as the years passed, he grew in height and his physical appearance radically changed. If you held a picture of Penn when he was age three next to a picture of him fifty years later, you would think it was a different person. But it's not. He's the same soul. He is still the same Penn Jillette that he was when he was three. He has simply grown physically and gained knowledge and experience.

The soul is the invisible life force that inhabits his changing body. It's his colorful personality, his character. It's what makes his brain think, his eyes see, his tongue speak, and his hands move. When Penn passes on, his brain will no longer register as being alive. His eyes will no longer see, nor will his tongue speak. This is because the life force that was within his body—the soul—has "passed on" into eternity.

TACKLING PENN

For the next few minutes we talked again about the banana routine. I wanted to move away from such trivialities and talk to him about his salvation, so I said, "Why don't you and I sit down and have a talk? I really appreciate talking to you." When he said that he was unqualified to speak with me, I said he certainly was qualified. Paul pulled the conversation back to the routine, saying that they were both *really* interested in it. They wanted me to explain why it was funny. I said, "It's just funny... I didn't know I was going to get interrogated for years about it; it was just a routine... People have never thought about a banana in that way before, and it gives them another angle to look at."

I then changed the subject. I said, "I want to thank you for that little video you made about a guy who gave you a Gideon Bible."

PENN: Oh yes, I believe that.

RAY: That was the most perceptive thing I've ever heard from any atheist or even non-Christian.

PENN: Oh, I don't think it's quite that, but...

RAY: It almost brought me to tears, it was so wonderful.

PENN: Well, thank you.

RAY: It's meant a lot to so many.

PAUL PROVENZA: What's the gist of that?

PENN: It's a thing where a guy comes up to me and I said many atheists don't think people should proselytize. And I said if you firmly believe that there is life after death and people are missing it, it is immoral *not* to proselytize.

PAUL: Right, right.

PENN: And I do believe that.

PAUL: Right.

RAY: *Penn, I'm tackling you tonight, because I love you.*

PENN: Okay. I don't really know what that means.

RAY: Because you said, "There comes a point [if a truck was going to hit someone] when you tackle a person."

PENN: Oh, yeah, yeah, yeah . . .

RAY: And that's what I'm doing, because I care about you.

PENN: Yes, I understand that, and I do agree with it and appreciate it. And the other part of it that has to be known is that the other side is just as sincere.

RAY: Yes.

After a few minutes of crossing swords, I decided it was time to go for the heart by addressing Penn's conscience. The Scriptures call the intellectual mind of man "carnal," and the carnal mind is in a constant state of enmity against God, particularly against His moral Law (the Ten Commandments —see Romans 8:7). This enmity can be seen in blasphemy, mockery of God, denial of His existence, and in contention. If I'm fortunate enough to "score a point" with one argument with an atheist, he will rarely concede. Instead, he will quickly grab another argument from his arsenal. I had to address Penn's God-given conscience (the place of the knowledge of right and wrong) if I was going to be able to give him the gospel.

The way to address someone's conscience is to open up the Ten Commandments, as Jesus did in Mark 10:17. In a sense we just read the law to the criminal to show him his guilt. An atheist may flinch at each commandment, but if his conscience is alive, it will convict him. The conscience is an impartial judge in the courtroom of the mind, saying "Guilty" or "Not guilty" as the prosecutor presents his case.

I was standing in as the prosecution, laying out the evidence for Penn to make a plea. It's up to him whether he will examine the evidence and be honest in his assessment.

As I began to do so, I was sure that he would shut me down. But to my surprise, he didn't.

RAY: Have you ever done the Good Test?

PENN: I don't know. I don't even know what it is.

RAY: Do you think you're a good person?

PENN: No. I don't think so.

RAY: So you've lied and stolen?

PENN: Sure.

RAY: Use God's name in vain?

PENN: Oh, [expletive] yeah.

RAY: Jesus said if you've looked with lust, you commit adultery in the heart. Have you ever done that?

PENN: Yes. That's nonsense.

RAY: So you've just admitted you're a lying, thieving, blasphemous adulterer at heart, and you've got to face God on Judgment Day whether you believe in Him or not.

PENN: No, I'm not going to.

RAY: Yes, you are.

PENN: I'm not going to.

RAY: As sure as Hell you will.

PAUL PROVENZA: You know, unless you believe, it's not blasphemy.

RAY: That's not true. Ignorance of the law is no excuse. Just because I don't believe in a law, if I break it I'm still going to face the consequences. And we've violated God's Law, the Ten Commandments.

PENN: Just because you believe in something doesn't make it real.

RAY: Now, do you know the other part of what I just told you? Even though we're heading for Hell, God is rich in mercy and He provided a Savior. You and I broke God's Law, and Jesus paid the fine. If you repent and trust in Jesus, God will dismiss your case because of what Jesus did on the cross. That's the gospel. He destroyed the power of the grave. *Man, I want you to find everlasting life with all my heart. I care about you.*

PENN: I know, I know. I believe that, I really do believe that. And you will give me the respect of not questioning my sincerity.

RAY: Yes, absolutely. All I ask is that you listen. I'm planting seeds; that's all. God makes them grow.

Then began a discourse about the issue of faith. It arose when Penn told me to embrace my doubts and I said that I didn't have any.

Just as the reality of the soul is denied by most atheists, so the word "faith" is denied because it is closely allied with the existence of God. Most atheists deny that they have any faith. So I asked Penn, "Do you have doubts about your wife's integrity? Do you have faith in your wife?" He replied that he didn't have faith; he had evidence. I said, "You don't *trust* her?" He did trust her completely, to which I replied, "Well, I trust God completely...So just as you don't doubt your wife's integrity because you trust her, I don't doubt God's integrity. There's no doubt at all. I *trust* Him."

Faith is an integral part of life. We couldn't live without it. Every human relationship is built on faith. It you tell a friend you don't trust him, then you have no basis for a mutual friendship. We trust pilots, doctors, surgeons, bankers, politicians, elevators, and a host of other things every day.

We then got onto the subject of the origin of DNA. When I pressed Penn about whether or not it made itself, he said he didn't know, adding that not knowing was a legitimate answer. I said that it wasn't: "If you said to me, 'Could a book make itself from nothing?' and I said, 'I don't know,' I'm copping out. It's impossible for a book to make itself from nothing, absolutely impossible."

While saying we don't know is an answer in many cases, it's not in this case. The Bible makes it clear that we *do* know that God exists, but that we deliberately switch off that light and hide from the truth in the darkness.

After our impromptu conversation, I was delighted at how it all worked out. God had given me the desires of my heart: I was able to share the gospel with Penn Jillette, who turned out to be one of the nicest atheists I've ever met. We have only looked at part of what was a wonderful conversation about things that matter most. I loved every minute of it, and thank God that He had opened this door *in due time*.

BRUSH WITH DEATH

Just after we got back to Southern California, we found that Lawrence had posted the photo of him and "Goofy" on his Facebook page, and Penn had tweeted his photo of the two of us to his over two million followers.

In his podcast, Penn later talked in-depth about the Lawrence Krauss interview, about our conversation on the sidewalk, and about something else. Minutes after I had told Penn that I was "tackling" him because I loved him, and reminded him of his analogy of a truck that was about to hit someone, Penn and Paul stepped into traffic and were almost killed. There was a loud screech of tires, and they came close to losing their lives as a car missed them by three inches.[61]

After Penn posted our picture together on Twitter, he was questioned about our meeting by Melissa Parker from *Smashing Interviews Magazine*. Here is a small excerpt from that interview:

MELISSA PARKER: You were recently in a photo with evangelist Ray Comfort who has a film called *The Atheist Delusion*. He says that he is convinced Hell is a very real place. Did he try to convert you from atheism to Christianity?

PENN JILLETTE: I only hung out with Ray for 45 minutes or an hour, and he was passionate, honest, straightforward and polite. I'd like to think I was the same. We disagreed. I think he's deeply wrong. I think he's also *tragically* wrong. It's easier to talk this way of seeing his point of view that there's a horror in the fact that I might be going to hell . . .

MELISSA PARKER: Have you ever second-guessed your atheism and thought that God may be real?

PENN JILLETTE: I try to intellectually think that all the time. I read the Bible. I talk to people like Ray Comfort. I try to be very, very open. But, I've got to tell you, the fear that others describe, the fear that I might be wrong and might be going to hell, I may have felt that way as a young child, but I can't remember in my adult life ever feeling that fear. I like to look at it intellectually, but I'm pretty happy with life the way it's going. I'm pretty happy with my friends and my family. I'm pretty happy with the love of the world . . . [62]

Penn's comments in this interview illustrate the paradox with this man: though he truly hates the Bible and mocks the things of God to the extreme, at the same time he speaks well of Christians. Seeing his reaction gave me hope that the hand of God is on this man. I'm also delighted that Banana Man had secular readers reading and thinking about God and the reality of Hell.

In the next chapter, we will look at something that I have never shared publicly. It's a wonderful key that softens even the hardest of atheists' hearts.

CHAPTER 11

A BASKET CASE

"But I say to you, love your enemies, bless those who
curse you, do good to those who hate you, and pray for
those who spitefully use you and persecute you."
—MATTHEW 5:44

The Bible says that when we do a charitable deed, it should be so secret that our left hand shouldn't know what our right hand is doing (see Matthew 6:3). When it comes to our personal giving, no one knows how much Sue and I give except God and our accountant. But I want to tell you what I do to demonstrate my love for atheists, to show you that Christians have a powerful weapon to reach those who are held captive by death.

I believe that a nice gift can speak louder to an unbeliever than the most brilliant apologetics. So after Richard Dawkins called me an "idiot" on CNN back in 2009, I sent him gift baskets along with my best wishes. I had one delivered to him in England, when we gave away a thousand copies of our special edition of *The Origin of Species* at Oxford University. When he went to Australia to speak in universities, there was another gift basket—with a banana and card—awaiting him. I wanted to show him that I cared about him.

Consider the words of Scripture, in 1 Peter 2:15–17:

> For this is the will of God, that by doing good you may put to silence the ignorance of foolish men—as free, yet not using liberty as a cloak for vice, but as bondservants of God. Honor all people. Love the brotherhood. Fear God. Honor the king.

We are to honor all people, and to love even our enemies, do good to those who hate us, and pray for those who spitefully use us.

We are to honor all people, and to love even our enemies, do good to those who hate us, and pray for those who spitefully use us.

In 2014, someone created a meme that said if God told me to, I would rape and kill my children. The person added my name and picture to his sick words (as though I had written them) and spread it all over the Internet. Since then I have had hateful comments and death threats on my Facebook page from very angry atheists who think that I said that. The "Atheist Forum" wrote about the meme being a prank and included another atheist's comment on it:

> For being a bunch of rational thinkers, you guys sure do fall for these fake screen shots from this guy all the time. His account was obviously hacked again. Stop slandering the guy, especially with something that is this awful. I get it, he is a delusional [expletive], and says

some pretty stupid [expletive], but he is smart enough to know not to post something like this. Beat him with facts, not this garbage.[63]

The writer then said,

Yet astonishingly some atheists disagreed—they thought that Comfort deserved it, even if it wasn't true! Mandy Harris responded to that first comment with: "Nah [expletive] him, even if it is [expletive]. He deserves as much [expletive] as people can give him, this [expletive] moron has influence and that's dangerous."

It puzzles me how one can propose that inventing vicious lies about a person because he "deserves" it can be considered reasonable, rational and attractive?

I did see grace in Comfort's response as he offered to pray for the person who wrote the meme. Whether or not you believe in the power of prayer, there is at least a kindness in his response that seemed lacking in the original meme and in some atheist responses.[64]

Our lawyers traced the source to a middle-aged atheist who owned a construction business in Chicago. Instead of suing him, I sent him a gift basket and wished him well. I preferred to show him love and forgiveness because his salvation was more important to me than my reputation. Some may understandably disagree with that, but I would rather have God fight my battles, if He sees fit to do so. (Not only that, but nowadays with sleazy lawyers, godless judges, and a biased media, not every case that seems a slam dunk is one, and it can end up very messy, costing an arm and a leg.)

When Jesus was reviled, He didn't threaten those who abused Him, but instead "committed Himself to Him who judges righteously" (1 Peter 2:23). He is our example, and we are called to follow in His steps (v. 21).

Scripture makes it clear about our dealings with the world. Look at Romans 12:19–21:

> Beloved, do not avenge yourselves, but rather give place to wrath; for it is written, "Vengeance is Mine, I will repay," says the Lord. Therefore "If your enemy is hungry, feed him; if he is thirsty, give him a drink; for in so doing you will heap coals of fire on his head." Do not be overcome by evil, but overcome evil with good.

Besides, I would rather win one soul to Jesus Christ than win one hundred court cases.

YES, THERE WERE NO BANANAS

I also did an interview with a couple of atheists on a radio show, where I knew that the female host held me in disdain. I was aware that she previously would say my name with the f-word in the middle of it. So after the interview I privately told her cohost that I wanted to send her a gift basket, and asked if he would trust me with an address. He did, and said later that when she got the basket and saw who it was from, she was speechless.

On his blog, he then posted a photo of the basket with the heading "Well, This Was a Pleasant Surprise," and said:

> You know, after panning Ray Comfort's anti-gay movie *Audacity*, and pointing out that his stars are actually supportive of LGBT rights, and describing the movie in painstaking detail during our podcast... you'd think Comfort would be unhappy with us. And then, yesterday, my podcast co-host Jessica received a lovely gift basket

from him. [Expletive], Ray, you make it very hard for us to criticize you when you do nice things like this! (In case you're wondering, there are no bananas in there.)[65]

Among the many comments there were mixed reactions:

I've been paying attention to Comfort for seven years. This is what he does. His niceness is part of his act. It isn't an isolated incident, he has a long history of it. If he wasn't an evangelist he'd be doing infomercials.

Why does a fruit basket make it hard to criticize Comfort? He's still a mendacious little twit, and his passive-aggressive "gift" doesn't change any of that.[66]

A PACKAGE DEAL

I occasionally search the Internet using my name along with the words "atheism" and "banana man" just for fun. On one of the videos I watched, I was horrified to hear the atheist hosts cussing me out big time.[67] It turned out that (unbeknown to me) one of my staff had erroneously filed a "DMCA" (copyright infringement) complaint with YouTube after the atheists had reviewed one of our movies. Apparently a complaint of this nature meant that they risked losing their YouTube channel. That was their source of income, and so they were very angry at me. The video had been made a full year earlier. Nevertheless, I sent them a gift basket along with a sincere apology.

The gesture blew them away, to a point where they made a nine-minute video called "Ray Comfort Sent Us a Package!"[68] It was such a pleasure to listen to what they said and then read the comments below the video.

Look at the effect of giving that token of honor and love. Here is a partial transcript of the video (cussing removed):

HUGO: Yeah, this is a little strange. This is a special episode because, as the title may have indicated to you, Ray Comfort, the Banana Man himself, friend of Kirk Cameron, and mustache aficionado, Ray Comfort sent us a package . . .

[They explained how my ministry had mistakenly "DMCA'd" them, and how I had made contact when I heard about it. He said, "And then the DMCA was lifted and we were good to go." He then related how a box arrived with a gift basket and a note that read: "Just saw your clip. Sorry for that false DMCA. You are welcome to review anything. Best wishes, Ray Comfort."]

JAKE: WHAT!?! And so inside this package, there's an array of goodies—which by the way, I got none of (laughter), because they were sent to Hugo, which is fine. But there's like a billion pears, some nice crackers, looks like chocolates. Some popcorn, some nice cheeses, some toffee maybe, or something? I don't know what you got, but also a basket with like, nesting materials in it, in case you wanted to nest.

HUGO: The basket itself is actually nice. I'm using it now for mail . . . Honestly, I'll give Ray Comfort this. We disagree on pretty much everything we could possibly disagree about. Like the creationism. The anti-science. The way he conducts his interviews. The way he edits them to make it look like he always has the upper hand. However, he did something wrong, by proxy through his company, and he apologized and sent us something. So, you got to give him credit for that.

JAKE: He owned it!

HUGO: That was good for him! That was nice!

JAKE: And, by the way, he gave us permission to review anything we want to review.

HUGO: Yep.

JAKE: Permission.

HUGO: Nice.

JAKE: I am very, *very* surprised at this . . . And, uh, honestly, if you want to contact Ray Comfort on Twitter or whatever, it's just @Ray Comfort, and say, "Hey! Good on you for sending an apology." He deserves it! He honestly does! I couldn't possibly say it any other way. The guy, for all indications—I've talked to Matt Dillahunty about him before and some other people in the community—and from all indications he's a genuinely nice guy, although he is very, very wrong about a lot of stuff. He is a nice person, and I care more about that than his opinions on things, which again are just incredibly incorrect. But that's cool, man!

This shows the power of demonstrated love. In the video I originally heard, they used every disgusting adjective you could imagine. The worst human being in history looked like a choirboy next to me. And suddenly I was Mr. Nice Guy—all because of a gift that expressed love.

Note again how the Scriptures explain what happened: "For this is the will of God, that by doing good you may put to silence the ignorance of foolish men" (1 Peter 2:15).

Consider some of the comments on their nine-minute video:

That's Christian! Good for Banana Man.

That's kinda cool of him to be honest. Kinda blown away to be honest.

Wow no kidding? That's . . . really refreshing honestly, and very big of him.

Wow, that's pretty cool of him. Not too many people would go the extra mile like that.

I never thought I'd say that Ray Comfort showed superior anything, but that was a classy move. Props.

Ray Comfort may be an idiot but he's actually a pretty nice guy from what I can tell.

Wow, that was really nice of him. I dislike him slightly less now.[69]

Despite our jousting about Heaven, Hell, and God, Penn Jillette had this to say on his podcast after our conversation, showing there was no offense:

I want to say, in fairness, Ray Comfort's very nice, very polite. I took a picture with him; very polite to me. He even sent a gift basket . . . Ray really has the politeness and kindness thing down.[70]

So if you are trying to reach that neighbor, or that non-Christian friend, or the antagonistic coworker, give or send them a gift. Don't put Bible verses all over it, "Praying for you" or even "God bless you" with it. Just say something like, "I thought you might like this. Best wishes." And then pray that God does the rest. You may not get to see the positive fruit I saw come from my gifts of fruit, but you will know that you did what God says to do, and that's what really matters.

CHAPTER 12

THE BIBLIOPHILE

*"I also have become a reproach to them; when they
look at me, they shake their heads."*
—PSALM 109:25

Hawks have a keen eye for any movement. They can easily spot a tiny rodent from a great distance and swoop in for a meal. In 2013, I made one small move, and in came the hungry hawks for a feast.

After 2012, my Facebook page had been invaded by atheists, as my blog had been earlier. *Thousands* of them. Many left nasty comments or horribly mocked God and the Bible, were extremely condescending toward Christians, and used disgustingly filthy, sexually crude language.

So I said that those who did these things would be banned. I explained the reason for banning: "If someone came into my house with filthy boots, stomped on our carpet, and mocked and insulted my family, I would show them the door and lock it."

Over a twelve-month period, I banned around five thousand who broke the rules. But many kept coming back. One changed his profile hundreds of times to get back in. It was like trying to have a picnic with my family and being continually attacked by swarms of biting mosquitoes.

In August 2013, an atheist who called herself "Leonie" said that there were contradictions in the Bible, and she gave what she thought were some examples. One verse said that no one had ever seen God, and yet the Bible in another place said that Jacob had seen God. I explained that this was called a "theophany," where God manifests Himself in some way, such as an angel, a burning bush, or some other form. But no human being has seen God, or can see Him and live. She replied, "As a bibliophile, I'm sure the gospels of John 1:18 and John 6:46 are familiar to you ..."

It was the first time I had ever seen the word "bibliophile," and I thought that Leonie had cleverly made it up to insult Christians. On first glance it looked like a cross between the words "Bible" and "pedophile." Atheists would regularly use made-up words like "Raytard" (a person who followed me, and was therefore retarded).

I wasn't even sure if "Leonie" was the polite female she seemed to be. This was because a male atheist had posted for many months on my page, using a photo of a pretty blond female as his profile picture, along with a female name. This had me replying to his comments with a little more courtesy than I would show a male. I believe that women are to be treated with a little extra respect (rarely would I stand up when a man walked into a room). Consequently, he was able to lead me on, no doubt all the while laughing up his sleeve.

Other atheists would pretend to be Christians and would say that I lacked love and shouldn't ban atheists. I learned to click on their profiles, which took me to their personal, blasphemous Facebook pages.

Catching the female-impersonating atheist left me skeptical about Leonie, so I firmly said, "One other thing. If you call any other Christian on this page a 'bibliophile' I will ban you."

She replied, "Ray I sincerely apologize for the use of the word 'bibliophile'. It means lover of books as I'm sure you know..." It was a silly mistake, and one for which I quickly apologized. I said,

> Leonie, I'm the one who should be apologizing. I thought it was just another atheist insult, a cross between pedophile and Bible. My sincere apologies. Still learning. Best wishes.

HAWKS SWOOP IN

After the apology, I didn't give a second thought to the incident. The kid had spilled more milk; just a typical day in my life, but not a train wreck. Not another thought...that is, until Richard Dawkins tweeted to his more than one million followers:

> Priceless gem! Ray Comfort insulted to be called a "bibliophile". Thought it meant pedophile! Oh joy![71]

Then Ricky Gervais, a well-known atheist actor and comedian, re-tweeted Richard Dawkins's tweet to around *ten million* of his followers, adding "Haha."[72]

Suddenly my little dumbness became breaking news for atheists. There appeared headlines like "Banana Man strikes again!" Even the "Friendly Atheist," Hemant Mehta, wasn't too friendly back then. He said,

> Whenever I come across a new word, I try to look it up
> ...it's a practice banana-man apologist Ray Comfort
> might want to adopt. On his Facebook page, Comfort
> posted a comment about Christians, the Bible, etc. His
> usual shtick. And then the following conversation actu-
> ally happened.[73]

He then linked his followers to the hard-to-believe conversation.

The *Urban Dictionary* had a new entry for "bibliophile":

> Mixing the words "Pedophile" and "Bible" together, ac-
> cording to the famous Banana Man; Ray Comfort.[74]

I had given the hawks a tasty feast. It seemed that everyone in the entire atheist community suddenly knew the definition of "bibliophile." It was the first word uttered by infants. "Honey, I just heard Timmy say his first word: 'Bibliophile'!" Everyone on earth—from Russia to Argentina, from presidents to peasants—all loved and used the word multiple times daily. Everyone, that is, except idiot Banana Man. I was bereft of even the slightest appendage of cognitive capacity. I had no choice but to capitulate and acquiesce to the fact that my dearth of cerebral currency took me to the very nadir of melancholic dolefulness.

There were comments like, "And on the 8th day God made Ray Comfort stupid," and, "This just reached a new level of stupidity." The Democratic Underground posted "Ignorant idiot of the week: Ray Comfort."

Some atheists, however, looked at the swooping hawks and showed a little pity on the rodent:

I'll give Comfort credit: He was gracious in his apology. I guess it's not too surprising that he thought two random things could be blended together like that. This is, after all, the man who believes in an intermediary between a crocodile and a duck . . .

Yes, he's not too smart, but you have to give him credit for admitting he didn't know what "bibliophile" meant. A lot of his peers would have tried to get out from under that.

I think many internet commenters could learn a lot from this exchange. A simple misunderstanding cleared up by genuine apologies and a willingness to back down over something effectively trivial. And not understanding the meaning of a word is trivial in fairness. I would certainly Google a word I did not understand, but I'm not likely to Google a word I think I understand. Fair play to Ray and Leonie, up with this sort of thing!

In Comfort's defense, I went to his Facebook page to refute something and he was very polite and patient. They did not block me like religious folks normally do. Of course, I was patient and respectful with my refutation—something atheists are terrible at, so it seems. Comfort has some incredibly irrational arguments about science but at least you can refute him and present evidence politely and patiently to get a positive conversation going.

I don't get why that's mock-worthy, sorry. There are one million words in English; we're all unfamiliar with some.

Even Leonie weighed in:

Ray's misinterpretation had me giggling all day Sunday but in fairness, after 4 hours (and plenty of joking at his expense), he apologized and left the post here. I award him very small levels of kudos for that. On a serious point though, this mistake has become a bit famous. Not quite Bananagate yet, but it's gathering a bit of steam. While I am really amused by it, I'm also a bit conflicted by the whole thing.[75]

If Banana Man was beginning to be laid to rest, he was resurrected on this day with a shout. It was one small misstep for a man, but a giant leap for atheist-kind. This was confirmation that Banana Man wasn't merely an entertaining clown, but an ignorant and uneducated one. Any possibility of gleaning a semblance of intellectual dignity was blown away in the winds of mockery.

My strong consolation was that this wasn't the first time a Christian had been used for entertainment.

As Banana Man, I had established myself as a reliable court jester. I was always good for a laugh. But my strong consolation was that this wasn't the first time a Christian had been used for entertainment. These toothless lions, however, attacked only with words. Nor did I feel the heat of Nero's flame. I had it easy.

A MEMORABLE THOUGHT

Richard Dawkins once said that he would debate me only if I donated $100,000 to his foundation. He considered me too dumb to dignify a discourse with him, other than to call me an idiot and tweet about my ignorance of the English language.

Despite my concern that I was less than a nobody in his eyes, I decided to send him a DVD. But I unwittingly gave him some more entertainment. It was more *bibliophile* material, and it was too good for him to pass up.

A man who visited our ministry told me that he was heading to Florida and that he planned to attend a Dawkins lecture. He asked if I would like him to hand-deliver anything to the professor. I grabbed a DVD of our "180" movie and jotted a quick note of greeting on the front of it. Then I forgot about it.

It wasn't long until I heard that Professor Dawkins had produced a selfie video about my note, and it was done with almost childlike excitement. Here is the short transcript:

> When I was lecturing at the University of Miami, I was approached by a little boy—must've been about seven or eight—after the lecture. And I thought, *How nice; a child has come to my lecture.* And he handed me a DVD which he said he had been asked to give me. And it turned out that he had been asked to give it to me by Ray Comfort, who will be known to many people as the Banana Man. And I looked at it. I was rather astonished to read the message on it. It was a very charming dedication to me. And I'll show it. He would like to hear my "thorts" on this.[76]

His "thorts" video provoked over 1,300 comments, most of which didn't exactly say nice things about me. Ironically, one of them stated:

What I find most disturbing about Comfort and others of his ilk is how easily and often they lie. I'm convinced they know Evolutiin is true, but they lie and deny it bcuz they're selling their dogma, and money is their true god.[77]

The professor was excited bcuz he thought that I didn't know how to spell the word "thoughts," and he had to share his excitement with his fans. As he spoke, he then held the "180" DVD up close to the camera so those atheists who didn't believe could see. This is bcuz, for an atheist, seeing is believing.

In so doing, he provided more material for my very public and ongoing stand-up routine.

The professor was so delighted he also sent out a tweet about it:

The same Ray Comfort is the original "Banana Man" bit.ly/1SCMs9 He also gave me a DVD with a request for my "thorts" about it.[78]

Still, I was delighted that the pope of atheism waved "180" up close and personal from his balcony. It is a very special evangelistic, prolife movie (which God has used mightily to save babies as well as save souls), and you can't buy such publicity.

As a Christian, be aware that the lost are also watching you closely, waiting to gleefully pounce on anything they can use to defame you and ridicule your faith. So whenever you are mocked and find yourself the butt of a joke, just "count it all joy" (James 1:2) and don't give it another thort.

CHAPTER 13

CASTING PEARLS

*"Preach the gospel, not with wisdom of words,
lest the cross of Christ should be made of no effect."*
—1 CORINTHIANS 1:17

L ate in the summer of 2016, we were filming open-air
preaching at a university for an episode of season five of
"The Way of the Master." I parked my car and made my way
toward the designated area. I wasn't sure exactly where to
go, so I stopped and asked a student for directions. He not
only gave me clear directions, he kindly offered to take me
to the area.

As we walked together, I asked his name then said I had
a question for him: What did he think happened after someone died—was there an afterlife? He said that when you were
dead, you were dead. It was all over. So I asked, "If Heaven
exists, will you make it there? Are you a good person?" He
said that he was. So we went through some of the Ten Commandments, and he admitted that he had lied, had blasphemed God's name, and had lusted after his girlfriend
many times. According to Jesus, he had committed adultery
in his heart.

He was reasonably concerned about the fact that if God gave him justice he would end up in Hell, so I shared the gospel with him. I explained that Jesus suffered and died to take the punishment for the sin of the world. We had broken God's Law and Jesus paid the fine, and that death had been defeated through the resurrection. I then said that God could completely forgive us and grant us everlasting life as a free gift upon our repentance and faith in Jesus.

As we rounded a corner, I saw our crew. I looked the young man in the eye and thanked him for listening to me, expecting him to brush me off with some short reply. Instead, he was clearly taken aback. He sincerely said, "No. No. Thank *you!* This has been *really* enlightening." The entire encounter took one to two minutes.

I then made my way toward the crowd that was listening to one of our team preaching and being heckled by a very colorful college professor. The heckler was an atheist, and obviously a Richard Dawkins fan. I love hecklers, so I was delighted that he suddenly turned to me and said that I was the one he wanted to speak with. Another gunslinger was in town.

After I got up on the soapbox, the professor and I fired shots at each other for about twenty minutes, during which time he tried to strengthen his argument by saying that he was once a Christian. So I fired back the same question I ask every atheist who says that he had once been a Christian: "Did you know the Lord?" To which the professor thoughtlessly fired back, "Yes, I did!" That's when I said, "I thought God didn't exist?"

Here is the dilemma for the atheist who says that he was once a Christian. A Christian is someone who *knows* the

Lord. Jesus said, "This is eternal life, that they might know You, the only true God, and Jesus Christ whom you have sent" (John 17:3). If an atheist says, "Yes, I did," he is admitting that God is real. If he says, "I *thought* I knew the Lord, but I didn't," then he was never a Christian. He faked it.

It would have been more biblical for the professor to say that he had a false conversion; he was like Judas Iscariot. Judas followed Jesus, but he was never a Christian. He was a pretender. Jesus said of him, "One of you is a devil" (John 6:70), and the Bible says that while Judas was the treasurer for the disciples he was stealing money from the collection bag (see John 12:6). Judas was a hypocrite. Those who profess to be Christians but never repent, and instead only pretend to trust the Savior, are just like Judas. And our churches are full of them.

After the professor left, a young man came to the microphone who said that he was a Christian. He then made reference to Matthew 7:6: "Do not give what is holy to the dogs; nor cast your pearls before swine, lest they trample them under their feet, and turn and tear you in pieces." His question was in reference to us preaching to gospel when there was contention in the crowd. Out of the hundred or so students gathered, about ten of them were very vocal and crude, mocking and blaspheming. I explained to him that I wasn't necessarily speaking to those who were mocking, but to the 90 percent who were listening.

One or two mocked particularly at the thought of Hell existing. Their reasoning was similar to that of the average atheist. If it turned out that Hell did exist, they would just deal with it. But Jesus warns us that Hell is a very real, and fearful, place: "Do not fear those who kill the body but cannot kill the soul. But rather fear Him who is able to destroy both soul and body in hell" (Matthew 10:28).

I shudder at the thought of any human being ending up in Hell. I can hardly entertain such thoughts. The apostle Paul said, "Knowing, therefore, the terror of the Lord, we persuade men" (2 Corinthians 5:11). If we care about the lost we must warn them about Hell. Colossians 1:28 says, "Him we preach, warning every man and teaching every man in all wisdom, that we may present every man perfect in Christ Jesus." Yet it's common for Christians to think that we are not to speak to those who mock or are contentious.

In one sense they are right. We shouldn't give the good news of Christ dying on the cross to those who only want to argue. But let me reason with you about this for a moment. The greatest "pearl" we preach is Christ crucified. The cross is the essence of the gospel. Christ on the cross is so essential to the message, Paul said, "For I determined not to know anything among you except Jesus Christ and Him crucified" (1 Corinthians 2:2). It is that pearl that we're not to cast before those who are contentious.

Remember that the preaching of the cross is foolishness to those who are perishing (see 1 Corinthians 1:18). So contentious, mocking atheists shouldn't be given the gospel. Like pigs with a precious pearl tossed at their feet, they will just trample on it as being worthless. Like Richard Dawkins, they won't see it as having the slightest value. To them it is nothing but foolishness. It's just part of the filth beneath them. As Dawkins said, the cross was "disgusting."

Instead of hearing the gospel, mockers need to hear the Law. When Paul spoke of "warning every man" he was clearly referring to the Law, not the gospel. The word "gospel" means "good news," and good news is not a warning.

The unrepentant criminal should be faced with his transgressions and the serious consequences of sin, not be told of mercy from the judge, because he doesn't think he needs mercy.

It is the moral Law (the Law of Moses) that connects with the human conscience and brings the knowledge of sin (see Romans 2:15; 3:19,20). The conscience, when it does its duty, then produces guilt. Guilt produces fear, and fear causes sinners to flee from the wrath to come.

And so when we preach, we first open up the moral Law, the Ten Commandments, as Jesus did in the Sermon on the Mount, to show our hearers the terrible consequences of their lawlessness. *Then* we preach the mercy of God in Christ. When they believe the message—that they are guilty of sinning against God—then the pearl of the cross will be valued. This is what Jesus told His hearers:

> "For if you believed Moses, you would believe Me; for he wrote of Me. But if you do not believe his writings, how will you believe My words?" (John 5:46,47)

The Bible says of the apostle Paul:

> So when they had appointed him a day, many came to him at his lodging, to whom he explained and solemnly testified of the kingdom of God, persuading them concerning Jesus from both *the law of Moses* and the Prophets, from morning till evening. (Acts 28:23, emphasis added)

The only time we should give up on any human being, atheist or not, is after they have breathed their last and are in eternity. It may be that the hate-filled, contentious, anti-Christian heckler is a Saul of Tarsus, whom God is about to save and use for His purposes. So don't let mocking (or the fear of it) keep you from speaking to the lost.

Despite having preached the gospel almost daily for over forty years, I'm continually plagued with fear when it comes to approaching strangers, and have to fight it every time. By way of encouragement, below are witness encounters I've had recently. These aren't for entertaining reading, but to help you become more confident and overcome your own fears of speaking to the lost.

MIKE AND HIS PIT BULL

I had determined to conquer my fears when it came to sharing the gospel with strangers, and had taken the Scripture "make no provision for the flesh" (Romans 13:14) and appropriated it to evangelism. My fear came from my sinful fleshly nature, and I wasn't going to make provision for it.

As I took off on my daily bike ride, I thought about how I had just pumped up the tires and what a difference it made to the speed of the bike. It was so much harder to ride if the tire pressure was even a little low. I applied that thought to evangelism also. Evangelism is so much easier if we are "pumped" to do the will of God, and the way to stay pumped is to think about the reality of Hell and the terrible fate of those we pass by.

There are not many people on the pathway on which I ride, so no one hears as I audibly cry out to God for wisdom on how to reach the lost. I had just been doing this when I saw a man in front of me, walking his dog. As I passed him I said a warm, "Good morning!" He responded just as warmly so I pulled my bike over about twenty yards down the path and waited for him to walk by. But he didn't. From the corner of my eye I could see that he was hesitating. Every day, people are mugged and robbed, and I was wearing a helmet, sunglasses, and gloves. I didn't blame him for hesitating, so I mumbled, "This is a bit weird," and rode on.

It was then that my conscience struck me. I was using that excuse to make provision for my flesh. So I turned around and rode back to the man.

As I approached him, I asked, "Did I give you one of these?" and handed him a coin with the Ten Commandments on one side and the gospel on the other. As he took it he said, "Be careful! He will protect me." I looked down at his dog. Yikes! It was the largest muzzled, most buff-looking pit bull I have ever seen up close and personal! I was so focused on the man that I hadn't even looked at his dog.

The air became tense so I said light-heartedly, "He's a big boy. What's his name, Fifi?" Neither of them smiled.

The man said, "His name is Bear."

"That's appropriate. My name is Ray." He told me his name was Mike, and he handed back the coin, saying that he would never read it.

Fortunately, I had another "weapon" in my arsenal. I have a small bag on my bike filled with evangelistic resources, from which I grabbed two Subway gift cards. "Well, I have another gift for you," I said. "Here, have lunch on me," and I handed him the cards—carefully, in case Bear wanted to have lunch on me.

Mike took them and said, "That's very nice of you, Ray," and the tension left the air.

"Mike, do you think there's an afterlife?"

"I don't know. I don't like to think about it because it's depressing. Death and all that."

"Yes, fifty-four million people die every year. If Heaven exists, are you going to get there? Are you a good person?"

"Yes, I think I am."

"How many lies have you told in your whole life?"

"About five."

"Have you ever stolen anything in your whole life?"

"No, I haven't."

"Have you ever used God's name in vain?"

"Yes."

"Jesus said that whoever looks at a woman to lust for her has already committed adultery with her in his heart. Have you ever done that?"

That's when Mike gave me his first smile. He was as guilty as sin when it came to lust, and he was concerned that, if he died in his sins, according to the Bible he would end up in Hell. And so I shared the gospel with him: that Christ died for sinners, taking our punishment upon Himself, and defeating death through the resurrection. I then encouraged him to repent of his sins and trust the Savior, thanked him for listening to me, and encouraged him to read his Bible.

As I left, Mike called out, "Really good to talk to you!"

JAKE AND ALICE FOUL MOUTH

As I rode my bike past one of my neighbors, I noticed that he was smoking a cigar as he stood on his front lawn with his two dogs. I had never seen him before and he looked a little intimidating. But so would a kitten, if I was planning to share the gospel with it. I stopped my bike, turned around, and asked, "Did I give you one of these?" As he took the coin, I explained, "It's a coin with the Ten Commandments on one side and the gospel on the other." He looked at it and said that he was brought up religious. When I asked him if he thought there was an afterlife, he said that he wasn't sure but that at sixty years of age he sure thought about it a lot.

At that exact moment, another neighbor walked by his house. He naturally called out to her, and the two of them carried on a conversation as if I didn't exist. I couldn't help feeling that there was a spiritual battle going on.

Alice came over to Jake and began telling him about her husband's knee operation and how much pain it was causing him. For the next fifteen minutes they talked about the pains of growing old, discussed the economy, and recited word for word the *Encyclopedia Britannica*. Or so it seemed.

I had never seen him before and he looked a little intimidating. But so would a kitten, if I was planning to share the gospel with it.

Both of them unashamedly used every filthy expression and cuss word you could imagine.

I decided that I wasn't going to be beaten and joined in the conversation, and discretely found out her husband's name and their street address.

When she finally left I got back to the conversation with Jake. He believed he was a really good person so I took him through the commandments. When I said, "Jake, I'm not judging you, but you've just told me that you're a lying, thieving, blasphemous adulterer at heart. On Judgment Day, are you going to be innocent or guilty?" He then came under serious conviction and said that he had to go. Suddenly the guy who had nothing to do but smoke cigars and stand outside with his dogs became as busy as a Wall Street stockbroker just before closing time.

I said, "Come on, Jake, give me thirty seconds." He did. That's when I said that he would be guilty before God. He then got really close to me and said that he had his own relationship with God and that it was personal, between him and nobody else, including me.

As he started to walk away I said, "Jake, I've got a couple of Subway gift cards for you here." That sure turned him around. He smiled as he took them and we parted in good stead.

I had decided to take a couple of my signed books to Alice's ailing hubby. I thought they would be appropriate for his age: *Hitler, God, and the Bible* and *The Beatles, God, and the Bible*. About an hour later I was a little nervous as I approached their door. There was an intimidating "No solicitors" sign on their fence, and I wondered if they too had a couple of pit bulls.

When the door opened, Alice was a little guarded. When I told her I was an author and had books for her husband, she asked which house I lived in. Mike then came to the door, so I inquired about his knee and asked if he would like the books. He did, and he extended his hand to shake mine. I signed both books and said that they were written in a New Zealand accent. That made him smile, and as I was leaving he said, "Do I owe you for these?" He didn't.

I'm sure glad I stopped to talk to Jake.

LARRY THE ROSE-SMELLER

I was riding my bike on my way home from our ministry when I saw the sight of an elderly man smelling roses. He was out for his perhaps daily walk around the block and still enjoyed the sweet fragrance of a rose. I ignored my fears, crossed the road, and pulled in between two parked cars. He was a little startled when I said, "Hello, sir. I see you enjoy the smell of roses. I have a gift for you." As he took it I added, "It's a coin with the Ten Commandments on one side and the gospel on the other."

He was congenial as he looked at the coin, so I asked, "Do you think there's an afterlife?" He looked thoughtful and said he believed there was. "Are you going to make it to Heaven when you die? Are you a good person?" He smiled and said that he didn't know, but that he hoped so.

I have a respect and an empathy for the tenderness of elderly people that makes it awkward for me to challenge them with the Law. It is far more comfortable for me to lay the weight of the Law on some smart-alec teenager, so with an elderly person I share it in a testimonial form. I said, "The way to find out if you're going to make it is to look at the Ten Commandments for a few minutes. Ask yourself if you have ever lied or stolen in your whole life, or used God's name in vain. When I realized Jesus said that whoever looks at a woman to lust for her has committed adultery in his heart, it suddenly showed me that I was in big trouble and I needed a Savior. It was then that I understood Christ died for my sins and rose again on the third day, and I needed to repent and place my trust in Him."

I asked him if he had a Bible and if he had been reading it. He said that he hadn't. I asked his name and then introduced myself. "How old are you, Larry?" He said that he was eighty-nine and that he needed to get right with God pretty quickly because he didn't have long.

"None of us do. Every day, a hundred and fifty thousand people die. This is so important, Larry. It's where you will spend eternity! You need to get that Bible out, dust it off, and read it daily. It's your food for your soul." Larry nodded in agreement.

I then gave him some Subway gift cards, for which he was grateful. I said, "Let me pray with you." He then came closer and I took hold of his trembling hand, and prayed with him, thanking God for Larry's openness, and praying for his salvation and health.

He said he read books, so I got his address and told him I would drop some off at his place. I grabbed *Hitler, God, and the Bible* and *Einstein, God, and the Bible*, a small booklet with principles of Christian growth called "Save Yourself Some Pain," and more Subway cards, and left them at his door.

I then drove my car around the block until I saw Larry. It was a sad sight. About half a dozen kids were walking past him as though he didn't exist. He was just some old guy with a cane, standing still until they had passed. I rolled down the window of my car and called out, "Larry! I left those books at your front door." He smiled and said, "Thanks again." I was glad I stopped. May God remind us that every elderly person is just a young person on whom time has left its mark.

RICHARD THE SKATEBOARDER

While riding my bike, I was following a skateboarder, who looked like he was in his early twenties, down a steep and narrow pathway. I followed him, readying myself to speak, when he dropped his skateboard and looked like he was about to hightail it out of there. That took me by surprise so I called out, "Did I give you one of these?" I scrambled in my little bike bag to find a Ten Commandments coin to show him what I was talking about. I finally grabbed one and gave it to him. "It's a coin with the Ten Commandments on one side and the gospel on the other. Do you think there's an afterlife?"

He said he didn't know, but he did think that Heaven existed. I asked if he was going there; was he a good person? Of course, as most do (see Proverbs 20:6), he thought that he was a very good person. So we went through the commandments. When he said that he had lied, stolen, blasphemed, and looked with lust, I asked for his name and said, "Rick, I'm not judging you, but you've just told me that you are a lying, thieving blasphemer and an adulterer at heart. Will you be innocent or guilty on the Day of Judgment?" He said that he would be guilty. "Would you go to Heaven or Hell?" Rick said that he would go to Hell, and that it concerned him.

I explained that Jesus suffered on the cross for the sin of the world, and that God could dismiss his case and forgive all his sins in an instant—"all those sexual fantasies that God has seen." I told him that as a young man, he has a choice. "How old are you, Rick?" He said that he was twenty-four. "You have a choice. You can continue enjoying the pleasures of pornography, fornication, etc., or you can repent and trust in Jesus and find everlasting life. The miracle is that when you do that, God will give you a new heart with new desires that long to do what is right."

I then asked him if he had ever lain in bed at night and heard his heartbeat in his ear and wondered what would happen to him if that stopped. He had. I said, "Guess how many people die every year. About eight hundred have died since we began talking. A massive fifty-four million die every year. Some are young, riding a skateboard. Other young people die from an aneurism in their sleep. This is more serious than a heart attack. Have you ever lost a loved one?" He had lost his brother a year ago. I asked if he had a Bible and he did. When I asked if I could pray with him, he said without hesitation that it would be fine.

After we prayed, he said, "Thanks for stopping me. I appreciate you talking to me." As he walked away, Rick smiled and said, "I'm going to have a better day now."

These were quick encounters but, God willing, they might affect someone's eternity. I hope so.

Why is it that as Christians we often fear sharing the most glorious news ever heard—that guilty sinners can find everlasting life? When you approach people in a friendly manner and explain the gospel in a way that makes sense (using the moral Law), you'll find they are almost always very appreciative and will often thank you. Once they see their guilt, they will greatly value and embrace the pearl of the cross.

CHAPTER 14

IF IT'S NOT YOUR KNEE

*"Behold, now is the accepted time; behold,
now is the day of salvation."*
—2 CORINTHIANS 6:2

I was in my late teenage years, heading for the beach with my beloved dog when he became excited and ran ahead of me across a road. I watched in horror as he was hit by a car, run over, and spat out the back. It was surreal, and I saw it in a kind of slow motion that I'll never forget.

I ran onto the road, picked up my precious animal, and held him in my arms. My brother rushed him to the vet, where it was determined that his injuries were so serious, he should be put down. That night, for the first time in my life, I thought deeply about God and about life and death. It was a wakeup call that would help to prepare me for my conversion.

My second wakeup call was my hernia operation. For some reason, I lifted a large rock when I was on a surfing trip. I was a fit and healthy, just-married twenty-year-old and had forgotten about lifting that rock until I felt a bulge on my lower abdomen. A doctor explained that I could leave it and risk it bursting and causing great pain, or get it fixed. I decided to have an operation.

As I was ushered into the hospital ward, I asked my nurse why a number of men were shuffling along at a snail's pace. She informed me that they had had hernia operations. I remember smiling slightly and thinking that I certainly wouldn't be doing the shuffle after my operation.

Fast forward half a day. I awoke after my surgery and felt that I needed a quick trip to the bathroom. I carefully turned to one side, slid off the bed and landed my feet on the floor. No problem. Then I lifted my right foot to take a step toward the bathroom *and felt an atomic bomb of pain explode in my abdomen.* I stood so paralyzed by the pain that I couldn't even do the shuffle! I had to wait for a nurse to help me get back into bed.

I realized that as a strong, vibrant youth, life could bring me to a helpless standstill. That knowledge was a powerful lesson in humility that I've never forgotten.

IT'S NO BIG DEAL

The host of a popular TV program once said that he wouldn't be hosting in the following weeks. This was because he was going to have a knee operation, adding, "And that's not a big deal—*if it's not your knee.*"

He was right. His knee operation was no big deal. People have knee operations all the time. But if it was *my* knee I'd be thinking differently. I would think, "Somebody is going to cut open my body and try to fix something that's not working. Will it be painful? How long before I can walk again?" A knee operation is a big deal, if it's your knee.

It's the same with death. While we may be sympathetic when someone dies, we're philosophical about their passing. Death is just part of life. After all, death happens to everyone, and "we've all got to go sometime." But when we personalize it, our death *is* a big deal! *It will be the biggest and most traumatic event of our life.*

Most people think they have no choice when it comes to making an exit. But the Bible calls death an "enemy" (see 1 Corinthians 15:26). That's good news, because it means that we can do something about it. We can surrender to it or defeat it.

When I was open-air preaching at a local college, a young man who was not a Christian stepped up to the heckler's microphone. After talking with him for a few minutes I gave him a litmus test. I asked him, "Are you afraid of dying?" He gave an immediate, "Yes! *Everybody* is." He was right. Everybody is afraid of death. The Scriptures tell us that:

Every human being is not only afraid of death, but is held in bondage by that fear.

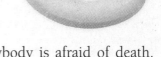

> Inasmuch then as the children have partaken of flesh and blood, He Himself likewise shared in the same, that through death He might destroy him who had the power of death, that is, the devil, and release those *who through fear of death were all their lifetime subject to bondage.* (Hebrews 2:14,15, emphasis added)

Every human being is not only afraid of death, but is held in bondage by that fear. The reason I ask people if they are afraid of dying is to do a humility test. It takes humility to admit that we are afraid of death. A proud person will hide it.

It is because atheism is rooted in pride (see Psalm 10:4) that the atheist will usually be quick to say he doesn't fear death in the slightest, "because I will simply go back to the state I was in before I was born." He will say that *nobody* knows what happens after death, and in the same breath will say confidently that *nothing* happens. In other words, *nobody knows but him.*

A MEMORABLE INTERVIEW

I had sometimes spotted a man named Jurgen standing on the outskirts of the crowd at Huntington Beach as we preached. But most of the time he would sit a little distance from us, with his shirt off, enjoying the warmth of the sun.

One day during mid-summer 2010, I asked him if I could speak with him on-camera. He was very congenial and said that would be fine. As we began the interview, he stated that he was an atheist, and when I asked him if he was a good person, he replied, "I've heard you a lot of times." So this wasn't the first time he had heard the gospel, but this time it was *personal*. We pick up the conversation halfway through the interview:

JURGEN: As far as I'm concerned, when I'm physically dead, I'm dead and that's the end of it.

RAY: What if you're wrong?

JURGEN: Then so be it. Why should I concern myself with that now?

RAY: Well, do you care about your life?

JURGEN: Yes.

RAY: You love living?

JURGEN: Yes, of course.

RAY: Jurgen, Jesus said, "If you look at a woman and lust for her, you committed adultery with her in your heart." Have you ever looked at a woman with lust?

JURGEN: I'm sure every man has at one time or another.

RAY: Yes, but have you?

JURGEN: Yes.

RAY: Have you used God's name in vain?

JURGEN: Yes.

RAY: Even though you don't believe in Him?

JURGEN: I think it's more a figure of speech.

RAY: He can wash away your sins so you're clean on Judgment Day, so that God can let you live forever.

JURGEN: Well, who wants to live forever?

RAY: I do.

JURGEN: I don't. I don't have enough money to live forever.

RAY: How old are you, Jurgen?

JURGEN: Sixty-eight.

RAY: How long have you got to live?

JURGEN: Probably another twenty years.

RAY: Are you afraid of dying?

JURGEN: No, not at all. If somebody told me, "You're going to die next month," I'd say, "Okay, I've lived a full life and I have very few regrets. So I'm ready to go."

[He then told me that he had a recent bypass surgery, and showed me a huge scar down the middle of his chest. So I challenged him with the thought that he let a stranger cut into his chest to fix his heart, just so that he could temporarily extend his precious life.]

RAY: Let me leave the ball in your court. Maybe tonight you'll have a minor heart attack on your bed and you'll think about the issues of life and death. And you'll say, "I'd better get right with God before death seizes me." This is so important! Remember, Jesus said, "What will it profit a man if he gains the whole world, and loses his own soul?" Hey, Jurgen, thank you so much for talking to me. I really appreciate it.

JURGEN: You're welcome. Have a good day.[79]

Bicyclist hit twice by vehicles dies
Dec. 23, 2010
HUNTINGTON BEACH – A 69-year-old man riding his bicycle was killed after he was struck by two vehicles Wednesday, police said. Jurgen Ankenbrand, of Huntington Beach, was pronounced dead at about 5:40 p.m. at the scene of the crash, police said.[80]

My heart breaks for the many Jurgens who boast of tomorrow, not knowing what it will bring. That dear man was riding his bike in heavy rain when he was hit by one car, then thrown into oncoming traffic by the impact and snatched into eternity.

God didn't give him the twenty years for which he was hoping. Perhaps he thought about our conversation after we spoke, and yielded his life to the Savior. I sincerely hope so.

THINK OF DAVID

The moment you stand up for the gospel, you too will be seen as a foolish "Banana Man" in the eyes of a proud world. You too will have to bear the scorn of the ungodly, and be perceived as an anti-science, low-intelligence, homophobic, brainwashed, witch-burning, pro-slavery, narrow-minded bigot who believes the ridiculous stories in the Bible.

But keep in mind that God not only uses foolish things to confound the wise, He also uses ordinary people to do extraordinary things. So, if you are like me—you are no-body special, but you love God—then step up to the plate. Plead with God to open doors for you to reach the lost.

Think of young David before he was anointed king. God instructed the prophet Samuel,

> "Fill your horn with oil, and go; I am sending you to Jesse the Bethlehemite. For I have provided Myself a king among his sons." (1 Samuel 16:1)

David was such an insignificant nobody that his father didn't even call him in from tending sheep so that he could line up with his brothers, when Samuel asked to see them.

But the LORD said to Samuel, "Do not look at his appearance or at his physical stature . . . For the LORD does not see as man sees; for man looks at the outward appearance, but the LORD looks at the heart." (1 Samuel 16:7)

Maybe you're not big, strong, gifted, good-looking, or rich. But your heart is after God. You love Him and you want to please Him. Like me, you are unspeakably grateful not only for the gift of life, but for the fact that you have been saved from the horror of death.

Think of Mary. She was just a young girl, who became pregnant outside the bonds of marriage and had to bear a social stigma because she carried the Savior.

We bear the same social stigma because of Christ in us. Not only is "Christ in you" our hope of glory, but He is the reason we are despised by this world. Consider these comforting words from Jesus:

"If the world hates you, you know that it hated Me before it hated you. If you were of the world, the world would love its own. Yet because you are not of the world, but I chose you out of the world, therefore the world hates you. Remember the word that I said to you, 'A servant is not greater than his master.' If they persecuted Me, they will also persecute you. If they kept My word, they will keep yours also. But all these things they will do to you for My name's sake, because they do not know Him who sent Me." (John 15:18–21)

So lift your head high and wear that humiliation as a badge of honor. Console yourself with the fact that the time will come when the first shall be last and the last first. On Judgment Day, those who are fools for Christ will be seen to be wise because they built their house on the rock. And tragedy of tragedies, those who seem to be wise by this world will be seen to be fools... because they spurned God's offer of Heaven, and by default chose Hell.

The Scriptures speak of this when they say,

> If you are reproached for the name of Christ, blessed are you, for the Spirit of glory and of God rests upon you. On their part He is blasphemed, but on your part He is glorified. But let none of you suffer as a murderer, a thief, an evildoer, or as a busybody in other people's matters. Yet if anyone suffers as a Christian, let him not be ashamed, but let him glorify God in this matter.
>
> For the time has come for judgment to begin at the house of God; and if it begins with us first, what will be the end of those who do not obey the gospel of God? Now "If the righteous one is scarcely saved, where will the ungodly and the sinner appear?" Therefore let those who suffer according to the will of God commit their souls to Him in doing good, as to a faithful Creator. (1 Peter 4:14–19)

Not only is "Christ in you" our hope of glory, but He is the reason we are despised by this world.

So never give up on the Jurgens of this world. The stakes are too high. Plead with them with passion in your voice. Let the Penn Jillettes and the Lawrence Krausses know that they may not believe in Hell, *but you sure do*. And because you love them you *will* tackle them. You will continue to warn them until they breathe their last and are taken into eternity to stand before the God they don't believe in.

Dear Mr. Comfort,
As a former atheist I want to thank you for never giving up on people like me. Through the grace of God I have come to realize that all of the previous beliefs I held were in blind faith, the very thing I once accused Christians of. It was I who was closed-minded and I have come to understand the truth of the Bible, God's Word. So once again, thank you and God bless you.
—Neil W., Texas

Thank you for reading this publication. May God bless you and your family, and use you in a wonderful way to fulfill His will.

NOTES

1 "Atheist Debate: BC/AD" <livingwaters.com/audio/assorted-messages/athiest-debate-bc/ad>.

2 Ibid.

3 Ibid.

4 Andy Butcher, "Atheists Invite Evangelist Ray Comfort Into Their 'Comfort Zone' in Orlando," *Charisma Magazine*, June 30, 2001 <tinyurl.com/jx5eluz>.

5 How it happened is detailed in the book *Out of the Comfort Zone*.

6 John Berman, Ethan Nelson, and Karson Yiu, "The Blasphemy Challenge," ABC News, Jan. 30, 2007 <tinyurl.com/2na6pe>.

7 Ibid.

8 Howard Kurtz, "Martin Bashir quits at MSNBC over Palin slur," Fox News, December 05, 2013 <tinyurl.com/j76cqls>.

9 To watch these and other Living Waters movies, see FullyFree Films.com.

10 "Kirk Cameron and Bananas," April 28, 2006 <youtu.be/2z-OLG0KyR4>.

11 Alex Murashko, "Christians Recruited to Battle Atheists on Facebook by Evangelist Ray Comfort," Feb. 26, 2013 <tinyurl.com/cblanpl>.

12 Bananas, Lies, and Ray Comfort," Apr. 2, 2011 <tinyurl.com/jp8morz>.

13 "I met Ray Comfort tonight," Pharyngula, May 5, 2013 <tinyurl.com/c4a9n4y>.

14 "Banana argument," Rational Wiki <tinyurl.com/jdh3s34>.

15 "Atheist Experience #702: Ray Comfort Interview," March 27, 2011 <tinyurl.com/zv3zrqs>.

16 "Ray Comfort Gets DESTROYED By Free Thinking Caribbean Woman," June 19, 2013 <youtu.be/pGjziqe_Zak>.

17 Steve Shives, "An Atheist Reads Ray Comfort," June 5, 2014 <youtu.be/oH_ui6C1bXA>.

18 "Ray of Light," *60 Minutes New Zealand*, Nov. 4, 2011 <youtu.be/pnLDkF7Yhs8>.

19 *Campbell Live*, May 23, 2006 <youtu.be/jYVwDMvnJ5g>.

20 "Banana Man & CrocoDuck Boy," Atheism TV, Mar. 1, 2011 <youtu.be/ug5xZ1fOr6Q>.

21 "Ray Comfort & Kirk Cameron The Banana Song 2.0," Sept. 22, 2010 <youtu.be/cvVgRcyZrjM>.

22 "Ray Comfort Interviewed by Brad Gurney," Feb. 26, 2014 <youtu.be/NrbaofH_XD0>.

23 *The Huffington Post*, Feb. 24, 2014 <tinyurl.com/knqm4g3>.

24 "Ray Comfort sketches 3," July 25, 2010 <tinyurl.com/zna8r8h>.

25 "Thunderf00t," Rational Wiki <tinyurl.com/z28cx2d>.

26 "The Thunderf00t - Ray Comfort discussion," July 24, 2009 <youtu.be/N2FskTKrx40>.

27 "Thunderf00t vs Ray Comfort - The Short Version," June 25, 2012 <youtu.be/QysfbldGVlk>.

28 "Reflections on Thunderf00t Ray Comfort discussion," July 25, 2009 <youtu.be/tOeW0TI5f3o>.

29 "Thunderf00t - Ray Comfort Discussion, Round 2!" July 22, 2011 <youtu.be/1Bn62F5pvp0>.

30 "Origin of Stupidity," Cristina Rad, Sept. 19, 2009 <youtu.be/fmHN3JtyUXg>.

31 Jim Emerson, "Kirk Cameron Combats Darwin in Bananaland," Sept. 23, 2009 <tinyurl.com/zc4wtea>.

32 "Don't Diss Darwin," National Center for Science Education, Oct. 28, 2009 <ncse.com/dont-diss-darwin>.

33 Robert Luhn, "Ray Comfort Is Bananas," National Center for Science Education, Nov. 30, 2009 <tinyurl.com/jgpzoju>.

34 "Foil the depraved designs of a dastardly duo!" Pharyngula, Sept. 17, 2009 <tinyurl.com/gsmrj52>.

35 "Dr. Richard Dawkins Mocks Ray Comfort (the Banana-Wielding Idiot)," Sept. 30, 2009 <tinyurl.com/zq6fgdp>.

36 "'Origin of Species' campaign enrages atheists," WorldNet Daily, Oct. 1, 2009 <wnd.com/2009/10/111563>.

37 "P.Z. Myers: Fearful Hypocrite?" Common Sense Atheism, Sept. 19, 2009 <commonsenseatheism.com/?p=3650>.

38 Democratic Underground, Nov. 18, 2009 <tinyurl.com/jtws9k2>.

39 Peter Wilkinson, "Dawkins: Evangelist an 'idiot' on evolution," *CNN*, Nov. 25, 2009 <tinyurl.com/yfhz3pd>.

40 "William Booth," God's Generals <godsgenerals.com/wbooth-2>.

41 "A Gift of a Bible," *Penn Says* episode 192, Dec. 9, 2008 <youtu.be/6md638smQd8>.

42 "Dean Dill Tonight Show," Jan. 22, 2008 <youtu.be/JNeFfOFJqEE>.

43 "Penn Jillette: An Atheist's Guide to the 2012 Election," Dec. 2, 2011 <youtu.be/kJGxVeQw3SE>.

44 Ibid.

45 "Richard Dawkins exploding at [expletive] in the Bible," Apr. 9, 2015 <youtu.be/FTXN5nOstRs>.

46 Ibid.

47 Charles Spurgeon, "The Offense of the Cross," Oct. 30, 1898 <spurgeongems.org/vols43-45/chs2594.pdf>.

48 Ibid.

49 Trevor Grundy, "Richard Dawkins Pedophilia Remarks Provoke Outrage," *The Huffington Post*, Nov. 9, 2013 <tinyurl.com/kqdl6gz>.

50 "Richard Dawkins defends the idea of having a mistress and lying about it," Uncommon Descent, August 21, 2012 <tinyurl.com/jtllygc>.

51 Richard Dawkins, "Abortion & Down Syndrome: An Apology for Letting Slip the Dogs of Twitterwar," Aug. 21, 2014 <tinyurl.com/jzax5bo>.

52 David Freeman and Eliza Sankar-Gorton, "15 Of Richard Dawkins' Most Controversial Tweets," *The Huffington Post*, Sept. 22, 2015 <tinyurl.com/j87egj2>.

53 Spurgeon, "The Offense of the Cross."

54 "Lawrence Krauss vs. Ray Comfort," Scott Burdick, June 4, 2016 <http://viyoutube.com/video/hQ31aMxZKYk/lawrence krauss vs. ray comfort>.

55 "Ray Comfort invites atheists to the creationist museum to talk," Sept. 29, 2012 <youtu.be/03roB2odNZE>.

56 See FullyFreeFilms.com to freely view Ray Comfort's films.

57 Penn Jillette's Sunday School, June 12, 2016 <tinyurl.com/gngowcs>.

58 See *The Beatles, God, and the Bible* by Ray Comfort.

59 Amanda Marcotte, "You're not fooling anyone with this stunt, Banana Man," *Raw Story*, Nov. 25, 2009 <tinyurl.com/h9p8kjl>.

60 "Ray vs Ra," Sept. 14, 2012 <youtu.be/8hoPb1ucSik>.

61 Penn Jillette's Sunday School, June 12, 2016 <tinyurl.com/gngowcs>.

62 Melissa Parker, "Penn Jillette Interview: 'Every Day, as Trump Gets Closer to the Presidency, I Get Sadder,'" *Smashing Interviews Magazine*, Aug. 2, 2016 <tinyurl.com/z3p6wn8>.

63 "That Ray Comfort meme," Atheist Forum, March 6, 2014 <tinyurl.com/q6ogox6>.

64 Ibid.

65 "Well, This Was a Pleasant Surprise," Friendly Atheist, July 17, 2015 <tinyurl.com/jcg463r>.

66 Ibid.

67 "Ray Comfort Took Down Our Video!" Aug. 27, 2015 <youtu.be/zDSZ8m0AQZs>.

68 "Ray Comfort Sent Us a Package!" Aug. 1, 2016 <youtu.be/6sqPHPkdtkA>.

69 Ibid.

70 Penn Jillette's Sunday School, June 12, 2016 <tinyurl.com/gngowcs>.

71 Richard Dawkins, Apr. 4, 2013 <tinyurl.com/jjpoblx>.

72 Ricky Gervais, Apr. 2, 2013 <tinyurl.com/hz3ulo6>.

73 "The Catholic Church Should Kick Out All Those Bibliophiles," Friendly Atheist, Apr. 2, 2013 <tinyurl.com/jxwtvy7>.

74 "Bibliophile," Urban Dictionary, Apr. 11, 2013 <tinyurl.com/hjey33u>.

75 "Good thing she didn't call him a pedagogue," Free Thought Blogs, Apr. 2, 2013 <tinyurl.com/hcbo6mr>.

76 "Richard Dawkins talking about Ray Comfort's DVD," Nov. 21, 2011 <youtu.be/HWIrnZizF7Y>.

77 Ibid.

78 Richard Dawkins, Apr. 2, 2013 <tinyurl.com/gps5jms>.

79 "I'm Thankful to MYSELF for my Life," Sept. 23, 2009 <youtu.be/F30lT5cflTw>.

80 Alejandra Molina, "Bicyclist hit twice by vehicles dies," *Orange County Register*, Dec. 23, 2010 <tinyurl.com/hszpss7>.

RESOURCES

P lease visit our website where you can sign up for our free weekly e-mail update. To learn how to share your faith the way Jesus did, don't miss these helpful resources:

Hell's Best Kept Secret / True and False Conversion: Listen to these vital messages free at HellsBestKeptSecret.com.

God Has a Wonderful Plan for Your Life: The Myth of the Modern Message: Our most important book (over 250,000 in print).

The Way of the Master Basic Training Course: This eight-week DVD course (based on the award-winning TV show) is ideal for group training in how to share your faith biblically.

What *Did* Jesus Do? Examine the way that Jesus, the disciples, and great evangelists of the past reached the lost.

School of Biblical Evangelism: Join more than 18,000 students worldwide—learn to witness and defend the faith in 101 online lessons. Also available in book form.

How to Bring Your Children to Christ...& Keep Them There: Biblical principles to help you guide your children to experience genuine salvation and avoid the pitfall of rebellion.

You can also gain further insights by watching the weekly *Way of the Master* television program (WayoftheMaster.com) as well as "The Comfort Zone" daily webcast program.

For a complete list of resources by Ray Comfort, visit **LivingWaters.com**, call 800-437-1893, or write to: Living Waters Publications, P.O. Box 1172, Bellflower, CA 90706.

THE
EVIDENCE BIBLE

"An invaluable tool for becoming a more effective witness." —FRANKLIN GRAHAM

Revised and expanded, *The Evidence Bible* arms you not just with apologetic information to refute the arguments of skeptics, but with practical evangelism training on how to lead them to Christ.

- Discover answers to over 200 questions such as: Why is there suffering? How could a loving God send people to hell? What about those who never hear of Jesus?

- In addition to thousands of verse-related comments, over 130 informative articles will help you better comprehend and communicate the Christian faith.

- Over two dozen articles on evolution will thoroughly prepare you to refute the theory.

- Dozens of articles on other religions will help you understand and address the beliefs of Mormons, Hindus, Muslims, Jehovah's Witnesses, cults, etc.

- Hundreds of inspiring quotes from renowned Christian leaders and practical tips on defending your faith will greatly encourage and equip you.

The Evidence Bible provides powerful and compelling evidence that will enrich your trust in God and His Word, deepen your love for the truth, and enable you to reach those you care about with the message of eternal life.

Commended by Norman Geisler, Josh McDowell,
D. James Kennedy, Woodrow Kroll, Tim LaHaye,
Ken Ham, and many other Christian leaders.